Copyright © 2024 Erson Goncalves

All rights reserved

No part of this book may be reproduced or stored in a retrieval system, or transmitted in any form or by any means, electronic, mechanical, photocopying, recording, or otherwise, without express written permission from the author.

ISBN: 978-1-0688736-3-8

R2

Cover: Erson Gonçalves

Acknowledgment

I am deeply grateful to God
for the blessings I receive.

The people who attend my lectures,
your presence inspires me

To my friends,
thank you for bringing me new knowledge.

A special thanks to Eline Anders and Ana Paula Gonçalves,
for their encouragement, collaboration,
and invaluable comments.

To my family,
for their moral support.

And especially to Jô,
my wife and lifelong companion, always.

Thank you all!

Erson

CONTENTS

Acknowledgment   3

Introduction   5

Part I – Sources of Conflicts   9
    1. External Conflicts   11
    2. Internal Conflicts   27
    3. Our Choices   31

Part II – Causes of Diseases   35
    4. Physical Disease   37
    5. The body speaks and writes!   41
    6. Psychosomatic Disorder   61

Part III – The Cycle of Forgiveness   73
    7. Moral Evolution   73
    8. Components of the Cycle of Forgiveness   79
    9. Triggering Event and Distancing   83
    10. Regeneration   89
    11. Reparation   97
    12. Meditation   103
    13. Self-Forgiveness   115

Part IV - Conclusions   123

Part V – Frequent Asked Questions   127
    And now?   135

Introduction

"If you have made a mistake, apologize...

Is it hard to ask for forgiveness?

Is it truly easy to be forgiven?

If someone has wronged you, forgive them...

Is it hard to forgive?

Who said repentance is simple?

- Excerpt from the poem "Not Everything is Easy" by Glácia Daibertsta

We often ruminate on bad thoughts about a certain unwanted situation. They keep going around in our minds, shedding no light on any solution. Feelings of anger, distress, and sadness surface.

"Learning to Forgive - A Matter of Health!" is a self-help book based on my experience. It aims to assist individuals desiring the freedom to live fully.

When we analyze the topics related to forgiveness, we notice they have a strong relationship with religious dogmas.

Biblical books, lectures, and prayers encourage believers to practice forgiveness. However, it turns out that both victims and repentant offenders have difficulty forgiving because the effective way "of doing it" is hard to understand.

This book delves into the understanding that forgiveness is a process of continuous learning that encourages self-discovery. The conscious practice of forgiveness is necessary to minimize negative feelings that affect our physical and mental health.

There were specific times in my life when I realized that something was holding me back. My soul was suffering from the pain caused by negative feelings that ranged from daily irritants to the most serious cases of offense. Perhaps the at the root of my hurt were prejudices, biases, and misleading messages gathered since childhood.

I felt trapped in captivity, not knowing how to deal with this situation, until I decided to come out of it and seek a solution.

The first step was to seek professional help. I began treatment with a psychoanalyst. He helped me identify the causes and find a solution to my suffering. Interestingly, I discovered that the solution had always been very close and depended solely on me. I just had to practice forgiveness!

After six months of treatment, I could forgive myself and reconcile with the offenders. Since my case was not so serious, the psychoanalyst discharged me with the recommendation that I continue reading self-help books and practicing meditation.

So, I became more interested in topics related to forgiveness. For over three decades, I researched dozens of books and attended many lectures on the subject, such as self-help, psychology, spiritualism, religions, health, and mental illnesses. I taught courses on the subject and received suggestions for writing.

After years of integrating this knowledge, my quality of life was gradually and consistently improved. To make it easier to memorize, I have grouped these teachings into a simple script divided into stages. I called it the "*Cycle of Forgiveness* ".

I have used the "Cycle of Forgiveness" at other times to overcome undesirable events of varying severity. Health comes first!

Since the results have been satisfactory for me, I have brought this knowledge to this book with the following proposal:

> a. To address forgiveness in the scope of physical and mental health.
>
> b. To help people minimize their suffering with the practice of forgiveness.
>
> c. To spread this knowledge so that anyone can transform themselves for the better, regardless of religion, level of education or creed.
>
> d. To show a path on how to forgive objectively through the Cycle of Forgiveness.

The body speaks and writes! Many diseases originate in the mind. Toxic thoughts and feelings emitted and received contribute to the materialization of diseases in the organs of the body.

The chapters that precede the description of the Cycle of Forgiveness summarize important knowledge for a good understanding of the reality of our day-to-day lives.

Clarifying the origins of external (social) and internal conflicts helps us minimize their effects. The conflicts generate synchronicities that affect us directly, as they alter the functioning of fluids, chakras, and organs, resulting in psychosomatic illnesses. Given the close interconnection between these elements, I suggest you read the initial chapters carefully.

The teachings in this book can assist you in clarifying, minimizing, or resolving sensitive situations and low-complexity conflicts.

Based on my experience, I emphasize the necessity of seeking guidance from mental health professionals, particularly in complex cases where their involvement is crucial.

The practice of self-forgiveness and other teachings will help you maintain consistent relationships with family, friends, and colleagues. You will enjoy life with more energy, more vibrancy, clarity, and a desire to love, knowing how to evaluate and defend yourself from potential risks of frustration. Remember that the success of the treatment depends on the patient's will and effort!

Happy reading, good practice and success!

Erson

Part I

Sources of Conflicts

Throughout our lives, we experience many situations of discord which, at more severe levels, can cause moral and physical suffering. Lack of understanding can cause conflict, which involves at least the following elements: the issue, the offender and the offended (victim).

The most common causes of external conflicts arise from friction brought about by the diversity of people in society, misleading messages, divergent human needs, and the clash of generations.

Internal conflicts can also make it difficult for someone to live in harmony with others.

Both external and internal conflicts are significant risk factors that can influence our physical and mental health. While these two types of conflicts are closely interconnected, this study examines them separately to better understand their distinct effects and dynamics.

1. External Conflicts

Diversity of people

We live among people with distinct personalities, behaviors, dispositions, and ways of thinking that lead us to adopt both defensive and offensive attitudes to survive. Our actions influence other people, and they influence us, whether it's in our families, place of work, social groups, or religious institutions.

We assume we are "normal people" and believe that others will respond as we would. The upbringing and moral rules received from our parents, relatives, educators, colleagues, neighbors, religious and cultural leaders, professionals, political authorities and social movements formed our individual frame of reference.

Besides valuable guidelines, individuals have also passed down inherited cultural traditions, prejudices, superstitions, and misleading messages that have influenced us and imposed fear.

Living in society, we need to be attentive to identify the signals that people send out to understand them and minimize potential conflicts.

According to Saint Augustine:

> *"People are not what they seem...*
> *People are not what they should be...*
> *People are not what we wish they were...*
> *People are exactly as they are*
> *and there is nothing we can do about it."*

This thought illuminates a direction for our lives. We cannot change anyone but ourselves. Trying to change others generates many conflicts, wear-and-tear, frustration and unnecessary suffering.

Conflicts often arise from factors such as aggression, baseless insults, rudeness, slow responses, and a lack of interest. Often, they have an underlying mental disorder that affects the behavior of the person, generating misunderstandings and conflicts.

Medical reports highlight various mental disorders. It is important to be sensitive to them to better understand people's unexpected attitudes and avoid conflict situations.

Anxiety. It is normal to experience occasional feelings of anxiety when faced with a dangerous situation, or when preparing for a challenging event, such as a job interview or public speaking.

When these feelings become frequent and overwhelming, the person may exhibit signs of excessive worry about everything and everyone, leading to stress and anger.

Depression. A serious mental disorder characterized by anguish, deep sadness, apathy, loss of interest in previously pleasurable activities, low self-esteem and feelings of guilt. In more severe cases, suicidal thoughts arise.

The intensity of the symptoms can be moderate, mild, or severe. They can appear soon after traumatic circumstances, such as the death of a family member or unemployment. It is important not to confuse depression with sadness, which is a passing emotion.

Grief. The suffering of grief brings an intensity of painful emotions that can cause depression, anger, guilt, and sadness. Sometimes the person needs to grieve, vent, remain in silence, or share memories. Listening is the ideal action.

Schizophrenia. It is a severe mental disorder (psychosis) that causes visual and auditory hallucinations, delusions, incomprehensible speech, and depressive symptoms. It manifests itself through exaggerated irritation in social and family relationships, inability to maintain a dialogue and withdrawal into oneself (isolation).

Bipolar disorder. A disorder characterized by extreme variation in mood swings. In the manic phase, the person feels powerful, and overly confident, performs many activities in a row, and sleeps little. In the depressive phase, the person experiences moments of inhibition, slowness in conceiving and carrying out ideas, as well as anxiety and sadness.

Alzheimer's patients. Alzheimer's disease is dementia that occurs when the brain's normal functions begin to deteriorate. Individuals with

Alzheimer's often prefer routine-bound and structure, and they may withdraw from social interactions, choosing to live in isolation.

They can be resistant to change and may have difficulty adapting to new situations. As the disease progresses, individuals typically experience a decline in their ability to manage daily tasks, becoming increasingly dependent on caregivers for support.

Drug addicts. Drug addiction occurs through increased frequency of use and the person's inability to resist the urge to use the product. To identify a dependent person, one can observe radical changes in behavior, relationships with suspicious people, marks on the body, changes in daily routine, and mental disorders.

Rogues (Scoundrels). Known for their deceitful and dishonest behavior, often engaging in fraud and swindling. They have little regard for conventional work or integrity, instead focusing on exploiting opportunities through methods like document forgery, manipulating outcomes, and other forms of trickery. Highly skilled and adaptable, they excel at quick thinking and deception, often blending into their surroundings. Their primary goal is self-preservation, carefully avoiding any evidence that could be used against them.

Psychopaths or sociopaths. Often referred to as social predators, thrive on manipulation and deceit, often causing harm to individuals, families, and organizations. They are highly calculating, ruthless, and unscrupulous, skilled at lying and charming others to serve their own interests. Lacking empathy and incapable of forming genuine emotional connections, they are devoid of guilt or remorse. Driven solely by self-interest, they can be aggressive and violent in their pursuit of personal gain.

To reflect...

1. Have you ever tried to change someone? Did you succeed?

2. Are you in a relationship with someone who has some kind of disorder? Describe the disorder and how you deal with that person.

Misleading Messages

We go through many unpleasant situations that are influenced by misleading or mystifying messages forged in our own minds.

Each person maintains their individual characteristics, their character, their way of being, and their way of seeing the external world. However, mystifying messages end up guiding our behavior and decision-making in a latent way. They stay in our mind, ready to act.

Adults need to understand that children's minds are like sponges that absorb almost everything. Therefore, it's important to exercise caution when interacting with them.

Powerful messages impress the mind and shape the ways of thinking, acting, and understanding. They influence other aspects of the person's life because they foment internal conflicts and even psychological disorders.

Misleading messages deceive or confuse others. They can be conveyed through words, texts, images, or objects. The intent is to exploit the gullibility of ill-informed persons, manipulating them into supporting the goals and interests of individuals or institutions in power.

Hoaxers aim to gain followers by creating confusion in people's minds to gain advantages. Their misleading messages are inconsistent and, to gain credibility with their audience, they refer to personalities, religious dogmas, superstitions, popular beliefs, folklore, "fake news", taboos and social norms. Hoaxers bet no one will investigate the veracity of their statements.

Today we are experiencing so-called "fake news", distorted official news and messages from dubious leaders. Any distracted person, regardless of their level of education, culture, or age, is subject to accepting and alienating themselves by these deceivers. They impose their ideas through fear and the fog they cast over the truth.

Security agencies recommend caution with phone calls from unknown people and with explosive news and propaganda. They recommend verifying the authenticity of any information and the credibility of those disseminating it. Online access makes it easier to identify phone numbers, as well as the identification of individuals and legal entities.

To reflect...

1. Do you feel bitter and don't know why?
2. Think about a belief or superstition that you believe in. Imagine removing it from your life. What might happen? Will you still miss it?

Human needs

According to Abraham Maslow's "Theory of Human Motivation," there is a five-level hierarchy of needs that human beings strive to meet, even if it creates conflict.

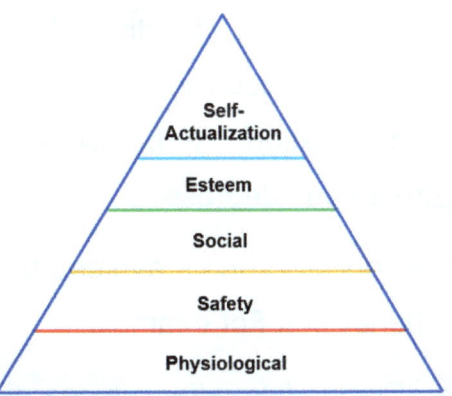

Physiological Needs. These are inherent to the physical body, such as hunger, thirst, sleep, sexual desire, shelter and basic sanitation. To satisfy them, people can even become aggressive.

Safety Needs. These include physical protection, employment, stable life, health, life insurance and laws to maintain order in society. Failing to meet these needs causes people to become apprehensive and insecure, and they develop syndromes of fear and danger.

Social Needs. In adulthood, social relationships emerge, including friendships with school and work colleagues, as well as the desire to love another person. The lack of social and emotional relationships makes the person depressed.

Esteem Needs. These are related to self-confidence, respect, appreciation, and prestige. The lack of recognition from others affects the individual's dignity, self-esteem and lack of enthusiasm for work.

Self-Actualization Needs. A person's ability to achieve personal goals in an area of activity. They generate autonomy, self-control, vision and individual independence. Despite all the effort, if the level of self-actualization is below expectations, the person becomes frustrated and depressed.

Many conflicts can be avoided by paying attention to people's moods and behaviors. For example:

- a. Demanding effective learning from a student who arrives at school very sleepy and hungry.
- b. After doing a hard job, the manager does not say thanks or recognize one's dedication.
- c. A young person feels depressed because their parents restrict the use of cell phones for social interactions.

To reflect...

1. *Consider each level of Maslow's pyramid.*
   Try to relate your current and future needs to the proposed scale.
2. *Which needs are priorities in your life?*

Generation Clash

Each generation brings its own perspectives, experiences, and aspirations for navigating life. However, a lack of understanding between generations can lead to conflicts, as differing values and attitudes often result in frustration, dissatisfaction, and tension between people from different age groups.

Marketing experts classify the population into groups according to date of birth, sexual orientation, and aspirations. For educational purposes, we can use this classification to understand the relevant characteristics of each generation.

Traditionalists. Born before 1945. Generation marked by difficult times, such as the Great Depression of 1929, World War II and the Korean War.
Orientation: Loyalty to lifelong employment and living under social norms.
Aspirations: Buying their own home.

Baby Boomers. Born between 1946 and 1964. The nickname refers to the large number of babies born shortly after World War II.

Orientation: Discipline, valuing work, family and individual progress. Rise of youth and cultural revolution.

Aspirations: Job security.

Generation X. Born between 1965 and 1980. The beginning of mass technology marks this generation.

Orientation: Demand for rapid adaptation to changes. Emphasis on learning. There was an increase in divorces.

Aspirations: Work to live. Balance between work and leisure.

Generation Y. Born between 1981 and 1996. Nickname "Millennials".

Orientation: Emphasis on the use of technology aligned with social causes and activism. Family formation depends on professional career and financial stability. Personal competitiveness. They have difficulty adapting to organizations with a traditional profile.

Aspirations: Freedom and flexibility at work to live better.

Generation Z. Born between 1997 and 2010. Nickname "Centennials".

Orientation: Digital and mobile generation. Frequently connected online. Emphasizes innovation and entrepreneurship. Learn quickly and ask a lot of questions. Activism.

Aspirations: Security and stability.

Generation Alpha. Born after 2010.

Orientation: The use of technology is more intense for both educational activities and entertainment.

Aspirations: Innovation.

Conflicts between generations occur because of differences in orientation and aspirations. Reflect on the following situations:

a. Traditionalist grandparents versus Generation Y grandchild.

> The constant insistence that the grandchild work, buy a house and start a family like their orientation in the past.
>
> The grandchild does not accept such a proposition because its priority is to focus on professional and financial aspirations, leaving the formation of a family in the background. These differences may generate constant friction in the family.

b. Baby Boomer parents versus Generation Z children.

> Daily control and friction with children because of excessive use of cell phones. Generation Z is digital, mobile and always connected to social networks. Teachers are also currently communicating with students online to carry out school activities, a method adopted during the two years of confinement because of the COVID-19 pandemic.

Controlling cell phone access can be challenging, even using control applications. When addressing this issue, it's important to proceed carefully, as excessive restrictions may lead to children becoming vulnerable or frustrated, potentially damaging their relationship with the family.

Influencers on social networks impose fashion standards and new ways of thinking to achieve sales objectives.

Young people with less discernment follow digital influencers. They accept those standards as correct. However, there is also a risk of narrowing the individual's view of other events that occur in his/her community.

Based on the sources of conflict described above, we can understand the complexity of the pressures and influences in which we are immersed. When our minds are filled with rigid thinking and negative feelings, there is a greater risk of discord and disagreement.

We need to be alert and mentally prepared to understand the present moment to avoid conflicts between people of different generations. These conflicts generate unnecessary stress and affect our physical and mental health.

Parents and educators should adopt friendly attitudes towards children and young people when establishing limits and responsibilities.

Avoid impositions and rigid attitudes, as was the custom in previous generations. We cannot demand from others what they are incapable of offering. Try to discover the talents of these new human beings to help them build their lives.

To reflect...

1. What generation are you from?

2. Considering your family group, what generation are your parents and other family members from?

Can you describe the characteristics of their respective generations?

3. Reflect on this statement:

"People don't leave their jobs; they leave toxic workplace cultures."

- Dr. Amina Aitsi-Selmi

2. Internal Conflicts

The struggle between emotion and reason is a key aspect of internal emotional conflicts.

We often hear people express their struggles, with the most common complaints being:

- Body pain
- Troubled relationships
- Financial difficulties
- Discouragement with life
- Bouts of sadness
- Feelings of guilt
- Inability to change bad habits

Patients come to their doctors and therapists in search of an immediate solution to their problems. In fact, treatment must begin with the patients taking the first step themselves.

Symptoms

The diagram below illustrates the groups of toxic and positive emotions. We are not inherently bad people; we simply desire to live well. Awareness is the key that guides our choices.

Toxic Feelings
1. Pride
2. Envy
3. Wrath
4. Laziness
5. Avarice
6. Gluttony
7. Lust

Good Feelings
1. Humility
2. Charity
3. Patience
4. Diligence
5. Generosity
6. Abstinence
7. Chastity

<- Consciousness

In the past, toxic feelings were called the "Seven Deadly Sins". Currently, scientists clarify that many of them are disorders that require treatment, without the feeling of guilt or sin. For example, people considered gluttony as both a vice and a sin. Today, professionals diagnose it as a compulsive disorder that can be treated.

We should avoid cultivating toxic feelings because they generate suffering, block progress, and lead to diseases. By cultivating good feelings, human beings grow and become happy.

Learning to forgive – A matter of health!

The following table shows the symptoms and a comparison between the two groups of feelings.

Toxic Feelings	Good Feelings
1. Pride Excessive self-love, selfishness, vanity, arrogance, haughtiness. Causes disturbances in personal and social harmony.	**1. Humility** Modesty, simplicity, respect for others, awareness of one's own imperfections, desire to achieve inner reform and spiritual progress.
2. Envy Strong desire to possess other people's property, low self-esteem, disrespect for other people's values, feelings of inferiority, difficulty recognizing the success of others.	**2. Charity** Feeling of compassion for others, doing good without expecting reciprocity, loving others, helping those in need.
3. Wrath Severe emotional instability, anger, violence, disrespect for others, desire for revenge, muscle pain, agitation, mental confusion.	**3. Patience** Tolerance, strong emotional control, calm, perseverance, love of oneself and others, moderation of one's own will, bearing hardships, acceptance.
4. Laziness Negligence, indolence, attitude averse to work and responsibility, indisposition, sedentary lifestyle, obesity, cardiovascular problems, lack of energy, slowness, laziness.	**4. Diligence** Proactive behavior, promptness, ethics, determination, commitment, zeal.
5. Avarice Greed, excessive attachment to material goods and money, passion for accumulating material goods, covetousness, fear of loss.	**5. Generosity** Detachment, donating of one's time, effort, or material goods, compassion for the suffering of others, selflessness, philanthropy.
6. Gluttony Compulsive eating, buying or using disorder, seeking compensation, difficulties in maintaining emotional control, obesity.	**6. Temperance** Abstinence, moderation in appetite and passions, detachment from people and objects.
7. Lust Attachment to sensual pleasure, selfishness.	**7. Chastity** Simplicity, abstinence, achieving purity of thought by education and inner renewal.

The detailed diagram below helps us describe our toxic feelings. We can overcome them by strengthening the opposite good feelings. Our consciousness is the key that controls this process of choices.

Toxic Feelings		Good Feelings	
Addiction	Insecurity	Abstinence	Humility
Anxiety	Irresponsibility	Acceptance	Individuality
Avarice	Loss	Affection	Joy
Anger	Laziness	Charity	Love
Criticism	Loneliness	Compassion	Lucidity
Cruelty	Low Self-Esteem	Courage	Naturalness
Dependency	Lust	Creativity	Patience
Depression	Pride	Detachment	Renewal
Envy	Repression	Diligence	Respect
Fear (Grief)	Rigidity	Forgiveness	Security
Gluttony	Selfishness	Freedom	Self-knowledge
Guilt	Wrath	Generosity	Understanding
Illusion	Worry		Wisdom

<- Consciousness

To reflect...

1. *Using the chart above, identify your toxic and good feelings.*

2. *Do you consider yourself capable of minimizing your toxic feelings and experiencing the opposite good feelings? Analyze.*

3. Our choices

We shape our lives through the choices we make. As we consider different options, various scenarios come to mind, influenced by both internal and external stimuli.

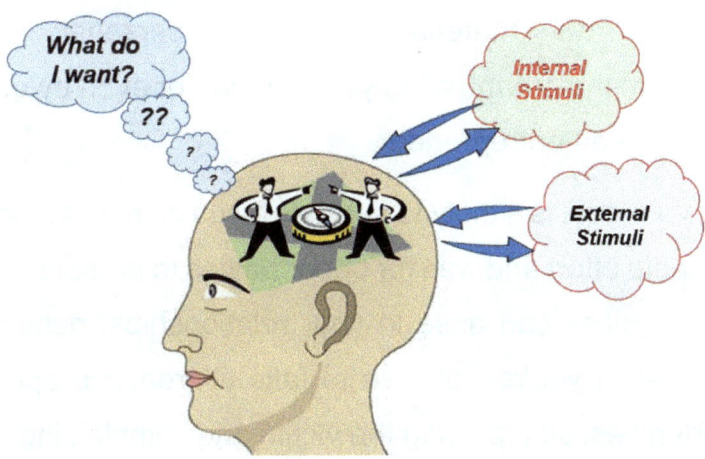

Considering this, we can reflect on the following three paths to answer the question: *"What do I want?"*

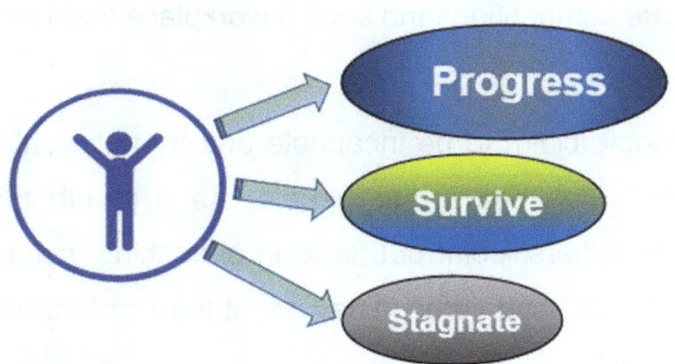

Progress. The decision to progress requires effort and commitment, as it is a constructive choice focused on growth and the cultivation of positive emotions.

By being proactive, you will find new opportunities, take on additional tasks, and be rewarded for your efforts.

Such rewards will materialize through personal satisfaction, recognition from the organization you work for, or even by gaining new clients if you are an entrepreneur.

Survive. If your goal is simply to survive, focus on maintaining your life with reasonable effort and wait for opportunities to present themselves. These opportunities can arise in your relationships, personal life, or work. However, if you're not able to take a proactive approach and seek opportunities, stop playing the victim and complaining that others aren't providing you with chances to improve.

Stagnate. If you decide to stagnate in life, do as little as possible, underestimate competition, and seek a workplace that keeps you from aspirations.

Stagnant people claim to be incapable and try to "push" their duties and responsibilities onto other people. As a result, they become dependent on others, point out flaws in everything, complain, blame God for "bad luck," and so on. They adopt the comfortable posture of "eternal victims."

No one escapes the divine law of progress that drives us towards our own development, whether today or in the future.

Self-forgiveness helps eliminate guilt and anger for having chosen undesirable paths. It restores hope of recovering a healthy life and reduces pain through increased self-esteem.

To reflect...

1. "What is your life's desire?"
    Try to answer based on the paths suggested above.

Part II

Causes of Diseases

Living beings can sense changes that occur in the environment in which they live and react through sensations.

Human beings get easily offended and feel uncomfortable by any external event that falls outside their context, that is, their "comfort zone."

This part of the book deals with aspects of moral evolution and physical sensitivity of the body and mind. It includes the causes of diseases, magnetic fluids, power centers, types of thought attunements and psychosomatic illnesses caused by emotional imbalances.

4. Physical Disease

According to the Michaelis Dictionary, disease (illness) is a biological change whose symptoms affect the entire body or parts of it, weakening the health status of the human or animal.

Several risk factors can contribute to changes in a person's health status. Changes in personal characteristics, behaviors and health status increase the likelihood of developing a disease or physical injury.

The organization EUPATI (European Patients' Academy on Therapeutic Innovation) classifies these risk factors:

Behavioral. It relates to bad habits, but individuals can often correct them through changes in behavior, such as:

- Inadequate nutrition
- Excessive alcohol consumption
- Tobacco and other addictive
- Physical inactivity
- Unprotected sex

- Not getting vaccinated
- Frequenting unhealthy environments
- Exposure to the sun without proper protection

Physiological. Related to genetics and lifestyle, these may influence the person's body, such as:

- Excess weight and obesity
- High cholesterol and glucose levels in the blood
- High blood pressure

Demographic. Related to the characteristics of the population where we live, such as age group, sexual orientation, occupation, religion, per capita income.

Environmental. These include social, economic, cultural, political, physical, chemical and biological factors, such as:

- Basic sanitation
- Clean drinking water
- Unhealthy or unsafe workplaces
- Chronic stress acquired at work (Burnout Syndrome)
- Air pollution
- Pandemics

- Violence
- Social behaviors

Genetic. These refer to the physical constitution (genes) of the person who causes diseases, such as muscular dystrophy and cystic fibrosis. The interaction of genes with environmental factors causes some diseases, such as asthma and diabetes.

Complementing these risk factors are infectious and parasitic diseases caused by bacteria, viruses, fungi and parasites. Many of them live in the human body and, depending on certain conditions, they can cause disease.

Some infectious diseases are transmitted between people, by insects, by animals, by the consumption of contaminated food or water, or even by the environment. Fever and fatigue are common symptoms of infections that, depending on their severity, the patient must go to the hospital.

Besides these diseases related to matter (the physical body), there can also be moral, mental, emotional and spiritual causes, which result in stress, discouragement, sadness, depression and other illnesses.

To reflect...

1. Analyze the risk factors mentioned above. Do you fall into any of these categories?

2. Do you consider yourself capable of minimizing or reducing the risk factors that may affect you?

5. The body speaks and writes!

The body suffers when the mind doesn't think!

The human body comprises a fantastic mechanism formed by physical, mental, and fluid components. They can interact in harmony depending on our thoughts.

Knowing how our body works, it is important to take care of it through traditional medicine or holistic therapies.

The human body has fluids and secretions. It holds about 70% water. Because of the concentration of mineral salts and impurities, this water becomes a good conductor of vital energy between the organs.

The body "speaks" through pain and "writes" on the skin the emotional reactions we emanate through facial flushing, irritation, goosebumps and allergies.

When we feel anger, hurt, sadness and guilt, we may be ignoring the consequences these negative feelings will have on the body, both in the short and long term. This is why forgiveness becomes a necessity directly associated with the health of the body and mind.

Internal imbalances generate most diseases. Thoughts start in the mind and become manifest in the body's organs. Human beings are sensitive to words, insults, and fears that trigger emotional reactions.

We become traumatized when we encounter something that makes a powerful negative impression on us. Trauma can be physical, energetic, mental, emotional, moral, social, toxic, climatic, sexual, and psychological. Thus, illnesses arise when any event "triggers" a trauma. An illness can manifest itself in the present or the future in various regions of the body.

The illustration below shows the set of systems in the human body. We can identify everything from the skeleton to the energy centers (chakras). It is important to note that all the energies in the body flow in all directions, magnetizing each organ.

Learning to forgive – A matter of health!

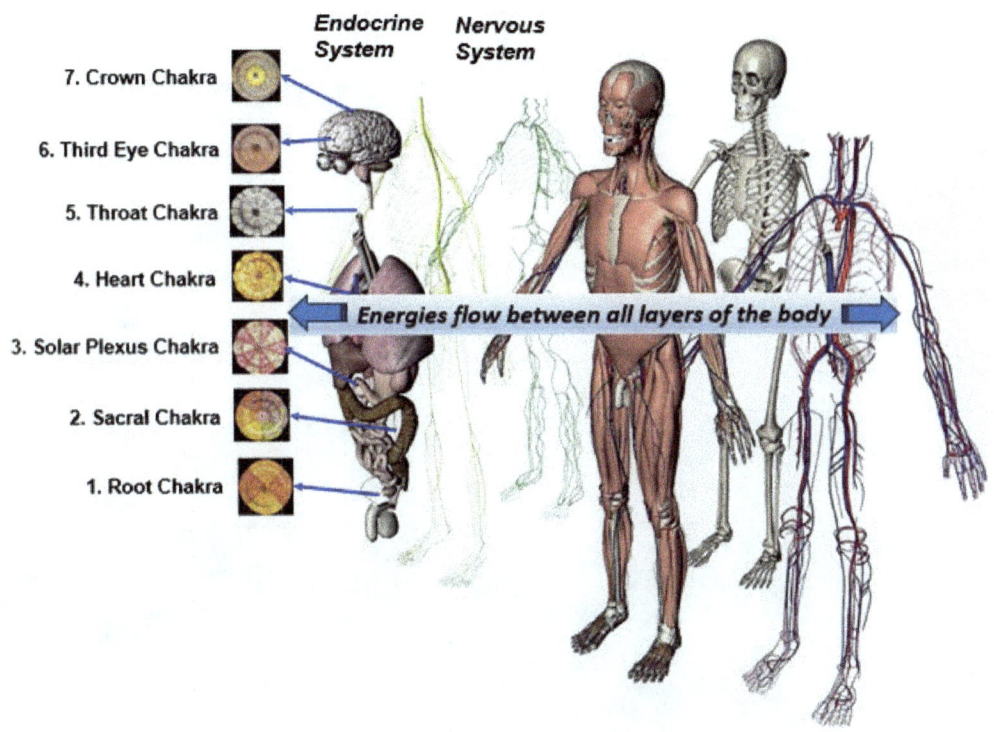

To reflect...

1. What am I doing to my body?

2. What has my body been "speaking" and "writing" to me?

Magnetic Fluid

All organic beings (humans, animals and plants) possess magnetic fluid. Living beings can transfer this energy between them, either in person or at a distance. Holistic therapies, such as prayers, Reich's therapy, blessings, and spiritual treatment, widely use the practice of energy transfer.

Scientists and researchers have studied and applied magnetic fluid for hundreds of years in the treatment of diseases.

Dr. Bernard Grad (1920 - 2010), a biologist and professor at McGill University (Montreal, Canada), was a pioneer in this field at a time when science did not recognize that some people had the power to heal, such as shamans and spiritual healers.

He was one of the leading researchers in energy healing through the laying on of hands. The results of his research laid the foundations and opened doors for work in energy medicine.

Dr. Wilhelm Reich mentored him at the university. Then, he adopted the master's ideas regarding orgone and vital energy.

Considering the organic and energetic processes of the human body, Reich's therapy treats the patient in an integrated and holistic manner, with an intersection between medicine and psychology.

Dr. Grad experienced the sensation of energy healing through the Hungarian healer Estebany. He encountered resistance in his research but continued his work on the quiet so as not to attract attention from the academic community.

He researched wound healing in mice, comparing the healing rates of mice cared for by a healer with those of mice not cared for by healer. The mice treated by the healer experienced significantly greater improvements.

He also observed the growth rate of seeds and plants that were watered with energy-treated water (fluidized water) by different people. He compared it to the growth rate of seeds and plants that received untreated water. There was a significant increase in the growth rate of seeds and plants exposed to fluidized water.

Dr. Grad concluded that when healing energy was involved, there was a dramatic difference in the positive outcome compared to experiments with no healing energy. He conducted this and other research from 1957 until the late 1990s (33 years).

To reflect...

1. Research online the work of Dr. Grad and Dr. Reich.

2. Describe the similarities between the work of these scientists.

Chakras

Chakras are the energy centers of the body, as illustrated in the diagram below. Each chakra connects certain groups of organs. They have acute sensitivity, and our thoughts and feelings influence them.

The human body has seven main chakras and 21 sub-chakras. Each chakra has a characteristic color and direction of rotation. When they are weak or deactivated, we notice symptoms such as malaise and headaches.

The **aura** is an energetic halo around the body which reflects our physical and psychic projections. Keith Sherwood recorded thousands of colors and shades of blue, red, green, brown, orange, violet, and white. The texture of the aura reveals the person's character, while the shape and color show their health and emotional state.

Below is a representation of how the human body integrates with the aura and the main chakras. The aura shows the person's mental waves. A bright aura makes up a shield against envy, jealousy, revenge and hatred.

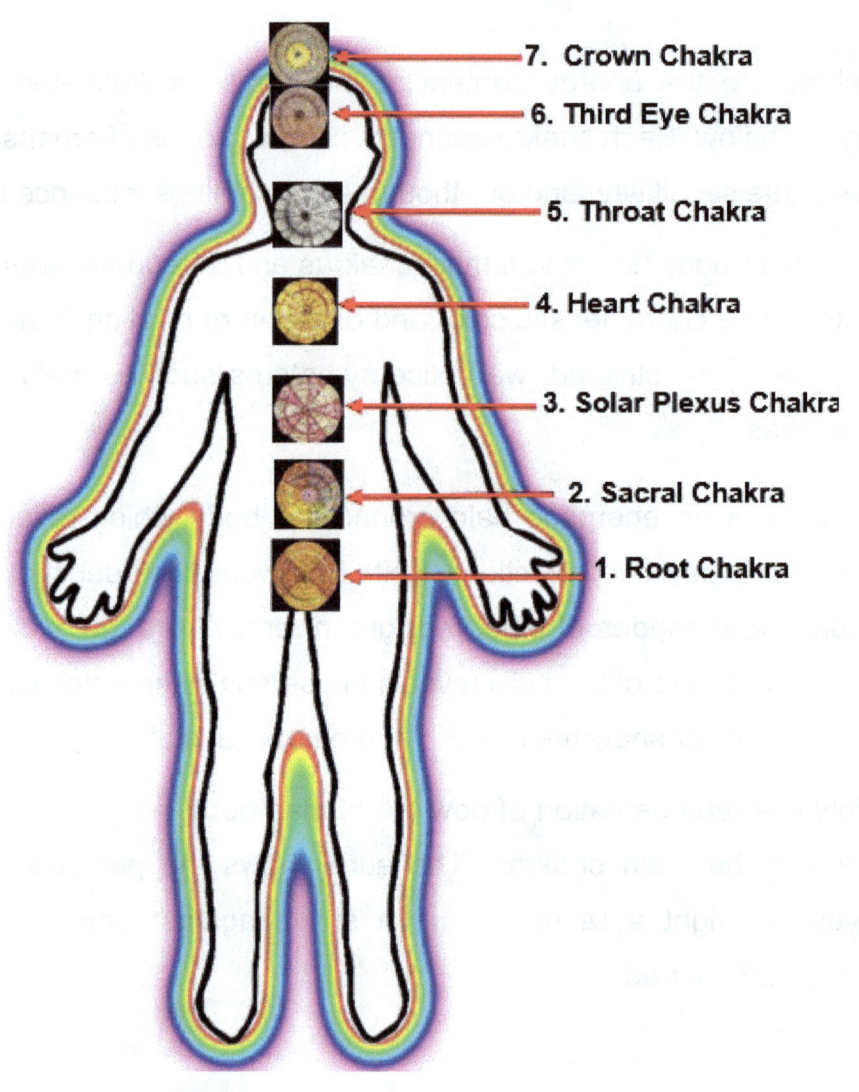

Learning to forgive – A matter of health!

Main Chakras
Source: *"The Chakras by photo Kirlian"* – C.W. Leadbeater

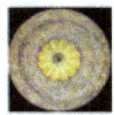
7. Crown Chakra
   Location: Pineal gland
   Connection: Universe, spirituality. It has the shape of a lotus flower.

6. Third Eye Chakra
   Location: Pituitary gland
   Connection: Intuition, wisdom, understanding, inner vision

5. Throat Chakra
   Location: Thyroid and Parathyroid Glands
   Connection: Communication, self-expression and judgment

4. Heart Chakra
   Location: Thymus Gland and Heart
   Connection: Compassion, friendship, affection, love and healing

3. Solar Plexus Chakra
   Location: Pancreas and Umbilical Region
   Connection: Personal power, ego, beliefs, fear and protection

2. Sacral Chakra
   Location: Adrenal Glands and Spleen
   Connection: Creativity, emotional balance, sexuality and relationships

1. Root Chakra
   Location: Gonadal Glands (Perineum)
   Connection: Reproduction, ambition, physical needs and survival

Sub-chakras

Besides the seven main chakras, there are 21 sub-chakras that act as sensors for the body.

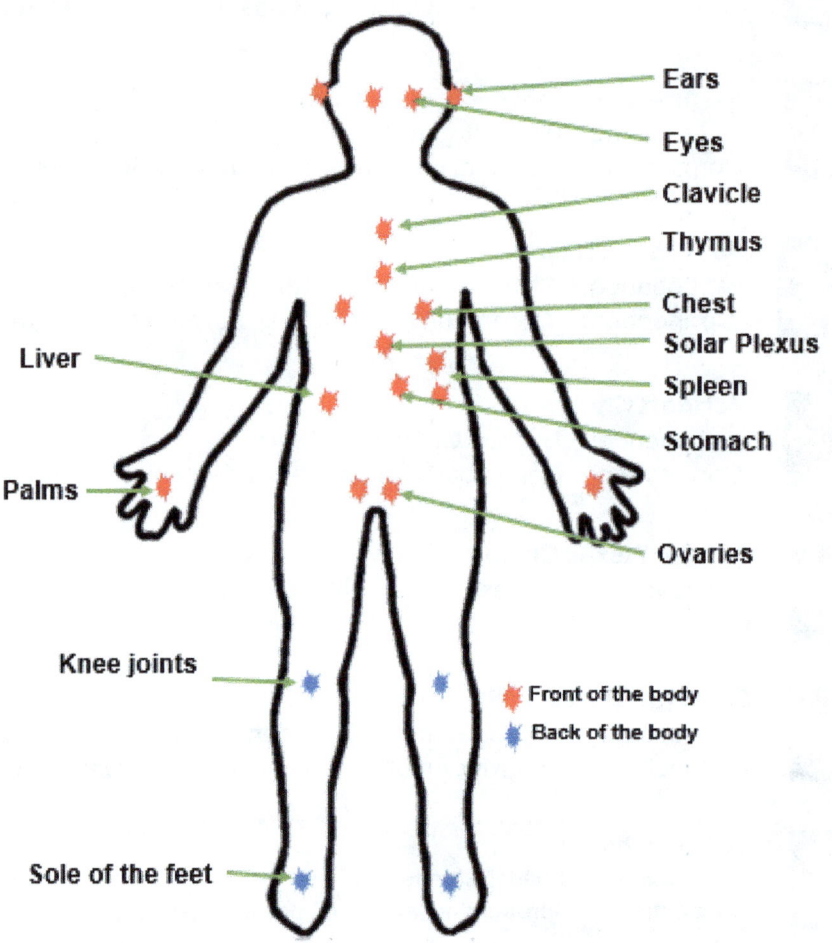

Ears. On the cheekbones in front of each ear. Under powerful emotion, they become red.

Eyes. The Third Eye Chakra connects to each eye from behind. The eyes connect our inner world with the outside, reflecting our true feelings.

Clavicle. The collarbone is below the throat. It is associated with the trachea and bronchi.

Thymus. Center of the chest. The Thymus relates to the Heart Chakra and plays a crucial role in the immune system of the entire body.

Chest. Above each breast, it connects to nutrition and our responsibility for our food choices.

Solar Plexus. Several glands, such as the pancreas, have a connection to the solar plexus region of the body.

Spleen. There are two sub-chakras connected to the spleen. They influence the balance of toxins entering and leaving the body.

Liver. Vital for the elimination of toxins and waste. It produces new chemicals needed to balance the functions of the other glands of the endocrine system.

Stomach. The upper and lower sides of the large intestine are associated with the stomach.

Ovaries. Each ovary or gonad has a sub-chakra that relates to the emotional aspects of sexuality and the level of fertility.

Palms. The palms of the hands are crucial for healing practices. Through them, we emit and receive energy.

Knee joints. Behind the knees, in the joint cavities. They are associated with certain fears, such as the fear of death, the fear of change, and the fear of losing control over the ego.

Soles of the feet. Their major functions include influencing contact with the earth and connection with the rest of the body. They receive the energy that keeps us grounded. They release unwanted energy and emotional waste.

To reflect...

1. Do you feel symptoms in your body, such as feeling unwell and having headaches frequently? Have you analyzed the reasons?

2. Have you been paying attention to your body's energy? What do you do to keep your chakras active and healthy?

Attunement

Human beings connect with the Universe and spirituality through the Crown Chakra, at the top of the head, which is connected to the pineal gland. The intensity of light emitted by the crown is proportional to our positive thoughts.

Thoughts bridge connections between people and other beings in the physical and spiritual worlds. But how do thoughts connect?

Thoughts are magnetic energies (fluids) that move through space like radio waves emitting short, medium, and long waves. Carlos Pastorinho (*"Techniques of Mediumship"*) teaches us about fluids and attunements based on physics studies.

The distance between wave crests and their respective frequencies characterizes the differences between waves.

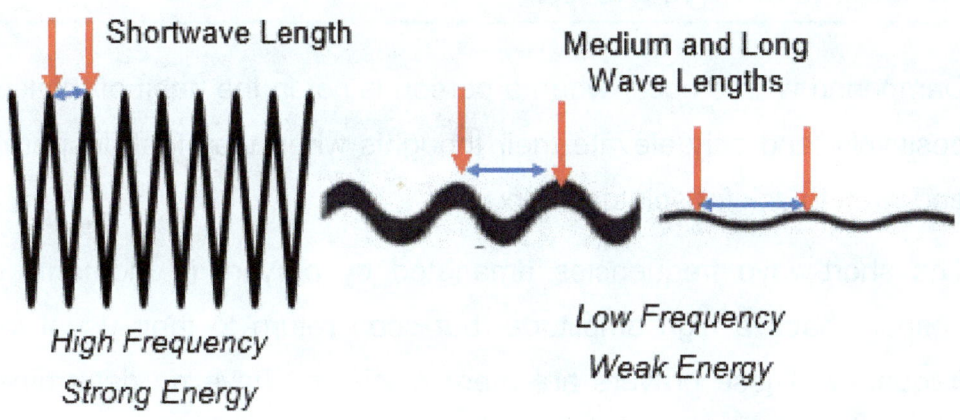

Short Waves
Higher-level thoughts

Through short waves, we emit positive energies of gratitude, praise, love, affection, etc. For example, fervent prayers evoke the highest spheres of spirituality when giving thanks, or for grace.

Medium and Long Waves Lengths
Low-level thoughts

Medium and long waves emit negative or indecisive attunement that ends up circulating at the level of the Earth's crust. For example, thoughts of revenge, hatred, sadness, guilt, hurt, resentment, intrigue and malicious comments about others.

Dampened Waves
Thoughts of varying levels

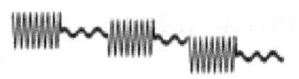

Dampened waves occur when a person is not in the habit of thinking positively, and only elevate their thoughts when they feel desperate and want to ask for spiritual help.

The short-wave frequencies emanated by prayers in moments of despair reach a high amplitude, but soon return to their usual low frequency. These prayers are mere noise and have no determined effect. These people often express their dissatisfaction with the lack of response to their prayers.

Blocking an attunement

When we notice undesirable attunements, we can block them by emanating intense emissions to counter them.

You have probably, at some point, found yourself in an environment that caused you to shiver, feel unwell, or have a headache. This occurs when the environment contains negative energy. Similarly, we may feel heavy-headed after talking to certain (toxic) people who seem to drain our energy.

To remedy this discomfort, temporarily distance yourself from the person or place. Elevate your thoughts through prayers or bring positive scenarios to that environment. Forgive everyone because they are unaware of the contamination of so much negative energy they carry. The graph below illustrates blocking of an attunement.

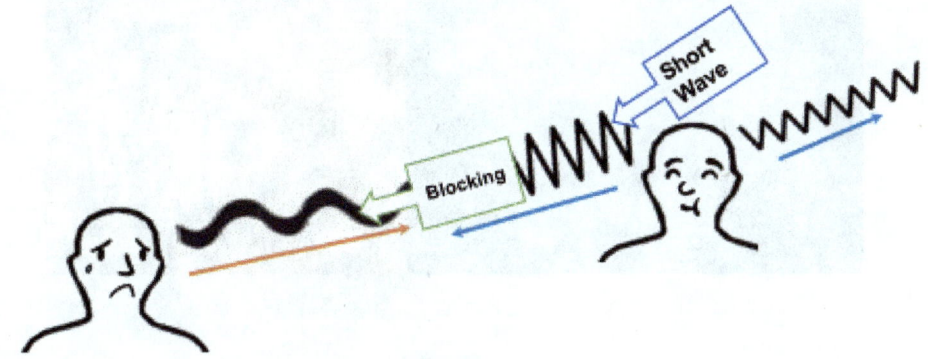

Observing harmony in water molecules

It is possible to prove that people are in tune with one another through experiments using water. Studies by Dr. Masaru Emoto (1943-2014), a Japanese scientist, prove that vibrations emanating from our thoughts and feelings alter water molecules.

The book "The Message of Water" contains interesting photos of water molecules that were frozen after being subjected to various situations during Dr. Emoto's experiments.

As an example, we reproduce two photos. The photo on the left shows the beauty of water subjected to positive messages of gratitude. In contrast, the photo on the right shows a water molecule subjected to messages of hate.

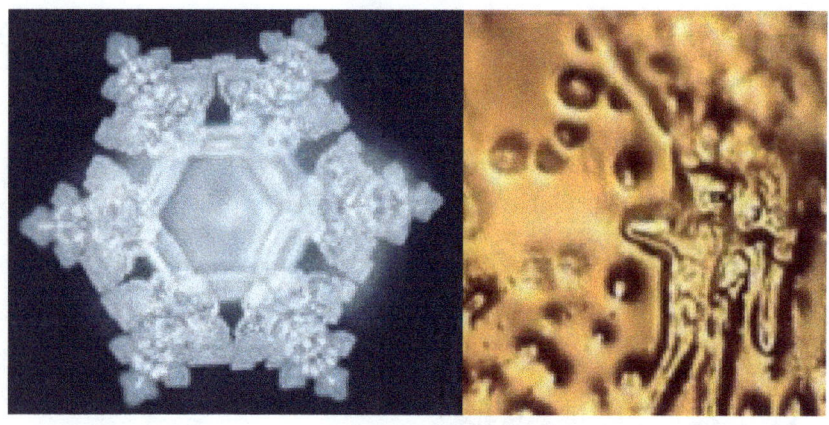

Dr. Emoto earned respect for proving that human thoughts can influence water molecules, despite the scientific community's skepticism.

One of his experiments can be done at home to verify his results without using any sophisticated equipment. Dr. Emoto used three containers filled with water and cooked grains of rice.

He labeled each container in the following manner: "I Love You", "I Hate You" and the third one had a blank label.

For a few weeks, he dedicated his attention to each container and verbally, emotionally, and physically expressed the message described on the respective label. The results were:

Container	Grain Status
"I Love You" Label	Natural fermentation
"I Hate You" Label	Moldy
Blank Label	Dark

This experiment provides the following insights:

1. Water molecules are good conductors of emotional energy.
2. Thoughts, feelings, and gestures emanate positive or negative vibrations. This principle applies to us, others, animals, and plants.

3. Vibrations transmitted through constant repetition promote either well-being or disease.

4. The human body holds about 70% water and forms an environment conducive to absorbing vibrations through the chakras and sensitive organs.

Therefore, we can conclude that the external messages, attitudes and vibrations that we receive daily can bring us healthy energies or harm the mind and body. They will also affect our thoughts. For example:

a. Messages that bring well-being:
Greetings, prayers, a fraternal hug, a friendly word, acceptance, positive phrases.

b. Messages that cause harm:
Shouting, rudeness, harshness, swearing, loud music, excessive noise, negative criticism and gossip.

To reflect...

1. What type of attunement do you use most during the day?

2. Do you feel comfortable using this attunement most of the time? Why?

3. If possible, do the experiment with cooked rice grains mentioned above. Check the result of your words and feelings.

4. Describe the effect of a loving message on a child. Consider if someone delivered that same message in a harsh tone.

6. Psychosomatic Disorders

Psychosomatic illnesses are emotional disorders that affect the functioning of the organs of the physical body. All layers of the human body, from the skeleton to the chakras, contain sensitive systems and organs that are magnetized by fluids. The latter have subtle sensitivity.

Originating in the head, the mechanism of emotions and feelings includes crucial glands for interacting with the rest of the body.

- ✓ Positive feelings bring feelings of satisfaction, pleasure, and well-being.
- ✓ Negative feelings bring feelings of discomfort and uneasiness.

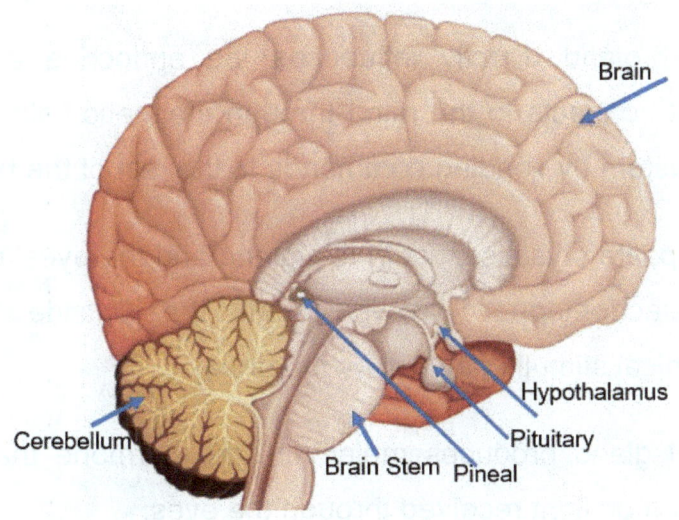

Hypothalamus gland. Produces hormones that are released into the blood and pituitary gland. Connects the endocrine and nervous systems by synthesizing the secretion of neurohormones. Regulates body temperature, feelings of hunger and thirst, sleep, and emotional behavior.

Pituitary gland. Below the hypothalamus. Produces important hormones for controlling other glands and maintaining the body's organs. These hormones act on the skin, bones, muscles, adrenal glands, mammary glands, kidneys, ovaries, testicles, and thyroid.

Pineal gland. In the center of the brain, it looks like a pinecone and is reddish gray. It is the size of a pea (adult = 5 to 8 mm). Through the pineal gland, we connect the biological structure of our body with the Universe.

The pineal gland directly influences the endocrine and nervous systems. It connects to the mind through magnetic fields and to the nervous system by sending commands to the rest of the body.

Identical apatite crystals exist in this gland and the eyes' retina. They convert electromagnetic waves from the outside world into neurochemical stimuli captured by the brain.

The pineal gland produces melatonin, the hormone that regulates sleep, based on light received through the eyes.

Neurons. Present massively in the brain, neurons are nerve cells responsible for propagating (transmitting) nerve impulses to the entire body. They also synthesize substances (neurotransmitters) that are secreted by the ends of the axons. The neurotransmitters activate other neurons and cells.

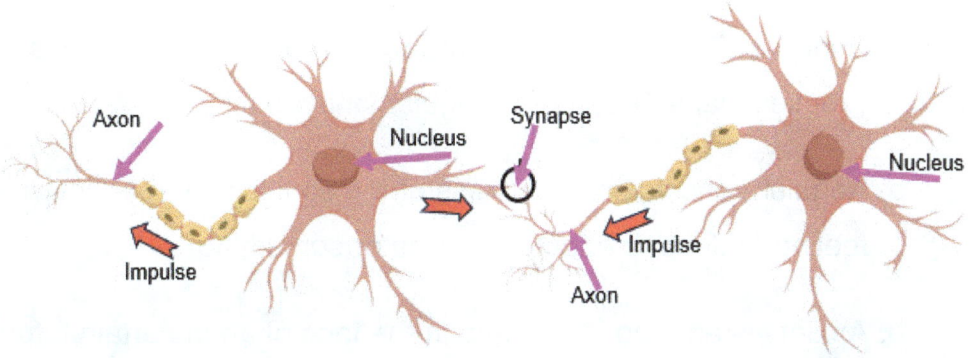

Source: Google Picture Free

The adult human being has about 85 billion neurons. Strong and systematically received messages form habits resulting in permanent paths of transmission between neurons through physical-chemical reactions.

Axons connect through synapses, which are the contact regions between neurons. Neurotransmitters transfer nerve impulses through chemical substances in the synapses and store them in the sacs at the ends of the axons.

Psychosomatic illnesses reflect emotional or psychological suffering onto the physical body. The term "psychosomatic" comes from the Greek words psyche (soul) and soma (body).

For example, trauma, psychological violence, stress, bullying and self-demand affect mental health and cause psychosomatic illnesses.

Intense moral suffering becomes evident through manifestations of distress, restlessness, bitterness, anguish and vexation.

    a. Anguish reflects great distress of the soul linked to an internal feeling of despair about someone or something.

    b. Anxiety is an emotional state in the face of an uncertain future in which the person foresees physical and psychological suffering with feelings of fear and apprehension.

    c. Guilt is the painful conscience of having failed to comply with a social or moral norm. It is taking responsibility for something reprehensible or harmful caused to another.

    d. Sorrow is the collected sadness we can see in one's face, brought about by regret, bitterness and disappointment. It is a consequence of resentment caused by an offense or slight.

    e. Anger is the state of mind characterized by irritability and bad mood. A strong feeling of hostility or antipathy towards a person or thing. Extreme irritation expressed through violent behavior, anger, fury and rage, motivated by hatred and outrage caused by disagreement between two or more people.

The most common symptoms of emotional instability are anxiety, pain, irritability, changes in appetite, fatigue, weakness, diarrhea and nausea, shortness of breath, tachycardia, itching, sadness, skin rashes and insomnia.

Common psychosomatic illnesses that materialize in the body are:

- Migraine – intense headache accompanied by vomiting, nausea and sensitivity to light.
- Gastritis – inflammation of the inner lining of the stomach.
- Gastrointestinal disorder with abdominal pain, constant diarrhea and constipation.
- Skin diseases: itching, redness, flaking, and rashes.
- Muscle and joint pain with no apparent cause.
- Sexual impotence because of psychological factors.
- Some types of cancer.

This is how the body expresses itself verbally and in writing. Expression of feelings varies with life experiences and context. Using a small rose leaf, we can understand how psychosomatic illnesses materialize in the organs of the body.

Let us suppose that when we are born, our soul is clean and healthy, like a green leaf.

As the years go by, we go through various trials that generate intense moral suffering.

Thus, anguish, anxiety, guilt, hurt and anger arise.

These pains strike the soul, like fungi that settle on a leaf, and the soul becomes ill.

Since the soul is close to the physical body, these "soul fungi" influence the organs of the body, leading to psychosomatic illnesses, such as:

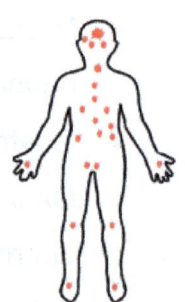

Migraine, gastritis, gastrointestinal disorders, skin diseases, muscle pain, sexual impotence and some types of cancer.

Taking Chinese medicine as an example, we complement the understanding of the relationship between feelings and organs:

Feeling (emotion)	Affected organ
Joy, euphoria	Heart
Sadness, melancholy, depression	Lung
Fear, panic	Kidneys
Worry, fixed ideas	Spleen

Anger, aggression, frustration	Liver

In her book "Heal Your Body," Louise Hay describes a list of illnesses that may have a mental cause. This is an interesting and recommended book. She describes each illness, followed by the probable cause and the new thought pattern to imprint new healthy pathways in the neurons.

For example, below are some types of illnesses from Louise Hay's list. Repeating positive thoughts can provide a cure for many illnesses.

Aging problems

Probable cause: Social beliefs, outdated thoughts, fear of being yourself. Rejection of the current moment.

New thinking: I love and accept myself at all ages. Every moment of life is perfect.

Alcoholism

Probable cause: The feelings of futility, guilt, inadequacy. Self-rejection.

New thinking: I live in the now. Each moment is new. I love and approve of myself.

Anxiety

Probable cause: Not trusting the flow and the process of life.

New thinking: I love and approve of myself, and I trust the process of life. I am safe.

Cancer
Probable cause: Deep hurt. Longstanding resentment. Deep secret or grief eating away at the self. Carrying hatreds.

New thinking: I lovingly forgive and release all the past. I choose to fill my world with joy. I love and approve of myself.

Colic
Probable cause: Mental irritation, impatience, annoyances in the surroundings.

New thinking: This child responds only to love and to loving thoughts. All is peaceful.

Depression
Probable cause: The anger you feel you do not have a right to have. Hopelessness.

New thinking: I now go beyond other people's fears and limitations. I create my life.

Headaches
Probable cause: Invalidating the self. Self-criticism. Fear.

New thinking: I love and approve of myself. I see myself and what I do with eyes of love. I am safe.

The Self-Forgiveness chapter provides the knowledge to ease the pain of the soul and the body.

Holistic Treatments

Holism (from the Greek holos = "whole")

In 1926, Jan Smuts (South Africa) coined this term in his book Holism and Evolution.

The tendency of Nature through creative evolution is to form any "whole" as being greater than the sum of its parts.

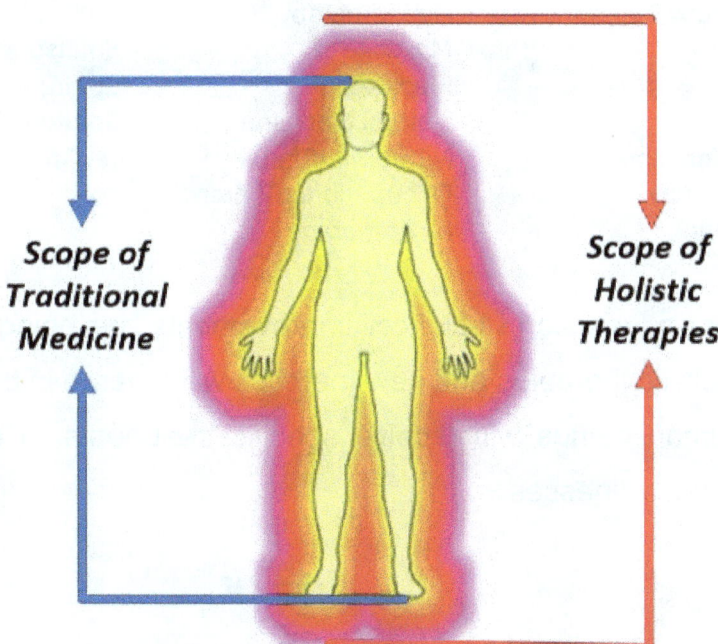

Principles of Holistic Therapy:

    a. See the problem holistically, not in fragments.

b. The emotional, mental, spiritual and physical elements form a system.

c. Focus on both the holistic cause and the symptoms of the disease.

In recent research, I found about 110 types of holistic therapies, including these best known:

Acupuncture	Holistic Therapy	Quantum Healing
Anthroposophical Medicine	Homeopathy	Reflexology
Apometry	Ho'Oponopono	Reiki
Aromatherapy	Hypnotherapy	Relaxation
Ayurveda	Massage	Shiatsu
Bio dance	Meditation	Spiritual Healing
Blessing	Natural Medicine	Spiritual Treatment
Chinese Medicine	Nutritional Therapy	Tai Chi
Chromotherapy	Occupational Therapy	Yoga
Healing Touch	Phytotherapy	

Because of advances in science, improvements are being made to existing holistic therapies and new methods will emerge in the coming years. Human beings will receive specific treatments to cure their psychosomatic illnesses.

To reflect...

1. *Have you ever experienced psychological violence, stress, or bullying? Have you overcome these traumas?*

2. *Do you suffer from distress, bitterness, anguish, vexation, or restlessness? If so, have you sought help?*

Part III

The Cycle of Forgiveness

7. Moral Evolution

Human moral evolution occurs through the intelligent effort to overcome challenges that arise during life.

Many people live lamenting their inability to minimize their pain. Unfortunately, they remain stagnant in their comfort zones and delay their personal evolutionary process.

The trials we go through during life help us develop and grow morally. We should understand them as a means of improvement. Overcoming them requires conscious effort fueled by the will to improve and by exercising one of intellectual capacity.

When we make efforts to change habits and attitudes, we gain new knowledge that we add to our existing understanding. Therefore, changes in attitudes are beneficial because they provide greater power of discernment and resilience.

We grow by embracing life's challenges. By noticing bad habits and striving to overcome them, the benefits of moral progress largely compensate for the effort.

We assume antagonistic positions with intensity proportional to our respective stages of evolution. Sometimes we are offenders and sometimes we are victims of others. Disputes are part of life. Offenders and victims have something in common: a pain that needs to be eased to continue living in peace.

Total forgetfulness of offenses is a utopia; we cannot erase them from our minds. Memory stores events that produce powerful emotions. The purpose of remembering these unpleasant facts is to avoid similar mistakes in the present or in the future.

When we commit a mistake, we feel a "guilty conscience" for having caused harm to someone else, or even for having transgressed a social or religious rule. A feeling of regret immediately arises, as well as the desire to rid oneself of the guilt by simply "apologizing," which may not always be the solution.

Asking for forgiveness is the responsible way to ease this painful feeling by obtaining mercy for the mistake committed. Forgiveness implies correcting the mistake and changing habits.

When other people offend us, we place ourselves in the role of victims and desire an apology from them.

Ability to forgive

It is common to hear people say that they cannot forgive someone or a group of people for some disagreement or unpleasant situation that occurred.

This difficulty in forgiving reflects human weaknesses, such as:

- Limited mental, emotional and spiritual capacity

- Difficulty identifying and recognizing one's own limitations

- Resistance to change because it requires personal effort

- Desire for others to solve one's own problems

- Desire to remain in the "comfortable" position of victim

These characteristics block the action of the soul in the mental field, inducing people to turn to material things that can bring immediate relief to their suffering. As a result, overcoming their pain ends up being postponed.

Forgiveness is one component of the group of good feelings, which also includes humility, freedom, acceptance, compassion, detachment and wisdom.

Overcoming hurt is based on forgiveness, and the ability to forgive depends on the severity of the offense and moral evolution of the victim and the offender.

Benefits of forgiveness

    a. It promotes release from suffering.

    b. It helps in the treatment of psychological disorders.

    c. It heals memories of painful experiences.

    d. It detoxifies feelings of guilt, fear, hurt, resentment, anger, frustration, and anxiety.

    e. It helps to identify bad or inappropriate habits.

    f. It helps to discover the reasons that lead us to play both the roles of offenders and offended (victim).

Reaffirming what I said in the Introduction, after years of adopting the knowledge of the practice of forgiveness, I noticed gradual improvements in the quality of my life. Since the results were satisfactory for me, I have brought this knowledge into this book with the following proposal:

    a. To address forgiveness under the scope of physical and mental health.

    b. To help people adopt the practice of forgiveness to reduce their suffering.

    c. To share the knowledge so that any person, regardless of religion, level of education, or creed, can improve themselves personally.

d. To offer the path of how to forgive objectively through the *Cycle of Forgiveness*.

To reflect...

"Minds that seek revenge destroy States, while those that seek reconciliation build nations.
As I walked out the door toward the gate that would lead to my freedom, I knew if I didn't leave my bitterness and hatred behind, I'd still be in prison."

- Nelson Mandela
(released after 27 years in prison for political reasons)

8. Components of the Cycle of Forgiveness

The knowledge gained in the previous chapters is useful for practicing the Cycle of Forgiveness.

The proposed process of forgiveness resembles the well-known figure of the snail shell. Starting from the center, where the event that generated the conflict occurred, ideas and attitudes gradually evolve.

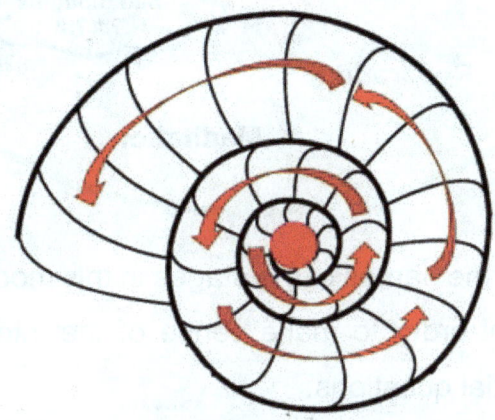

Being trapped in negative thoughts is like a prison without means of escape.

To live in peace, one must always seek reconciliation between oneself, and the people involved in the undesirable incident.

The "Cycle of Forgiveness", represented in the illustration below, facilitates achieving reconciliation. It deals with the process of conscious evolution in a sequence of steps that helps the person free themselves from the captivity of bad thoughts and feelings.

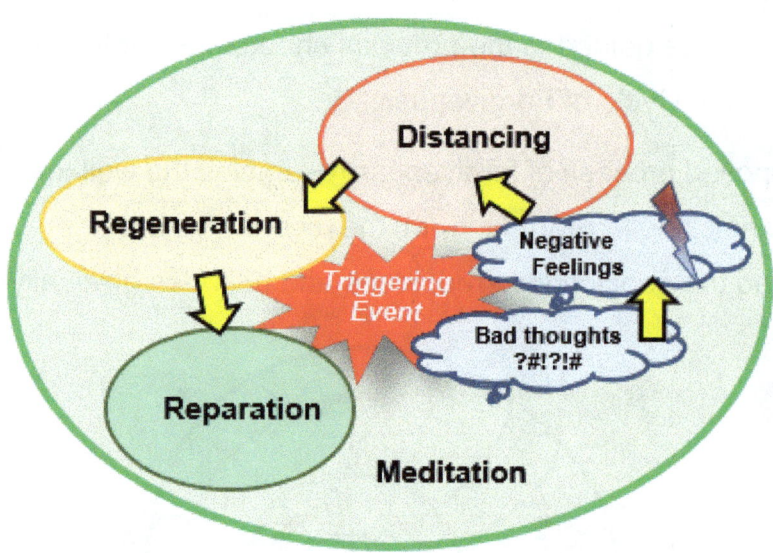

We already know the names of the stages in this model. I just put them together in logical order to make sense of the intended purpose of answering the initial questions:

"How to Forgive?" and

"What are the steps to forgive?"

This model is useful for both situations: whether we assume the position of the offender or the victim. During life, many offenders also regret and want to get forgiveness from their victims.

It is natural for us to resent any type of conflict that involves us. We become bitter, angry, frustrated, and dark thoughts arise in our minds. Depending on the severity of the problem, emotions are more intensely aroused by the negative situation.

Components

1. Triggering Event. Different ways may cause conflicts, such as:

- material temptation

- an impulse that instigated one party to insult the other

- disagreement or discord

- transgression of the law

2. *Distancing.* Physical and/or psychological distancing from the offender, the offended party, and the unpleasant scene. This can produce repentance by both the person who caused the triggering event and the person who feels offended.

3. *Regeneration.* This reconfigures physical and moral suffering, requiring a change in habits and attitudes.

4. *Reparation:* This minimizes the effects of the event that generated the problem by addressing the injury or damages and offering sincere apologies to someone.

5. Meditation is key to bringing all these components together. It accompanies the entire process until forgiveness and healing of suffering can occur, whether as an offender or victim of a situation.

These components interact with each other evolutionarily to replace suffering with positive changes in attitudes.

Throughout our lives, we encounter various events that cause suffering. The "Cycle of Forgiveness" applies to all events, past and present.

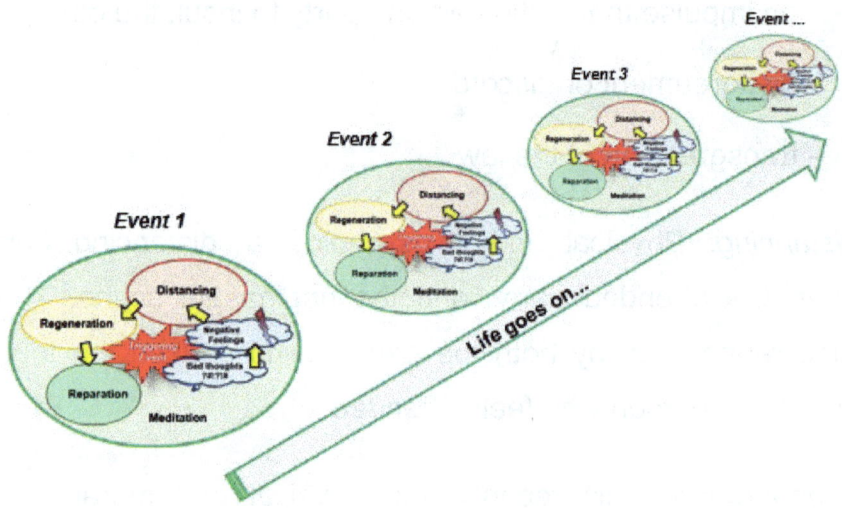

With experience, we gain more knowledge about the causes that gave rise to previous conflicts, as well as how to deal with each case. We keep events in memory precisely to prevent similar cases from occurring again.

This is the line of thinking that minimizes suffering.

9. Triggering Event and Distancing

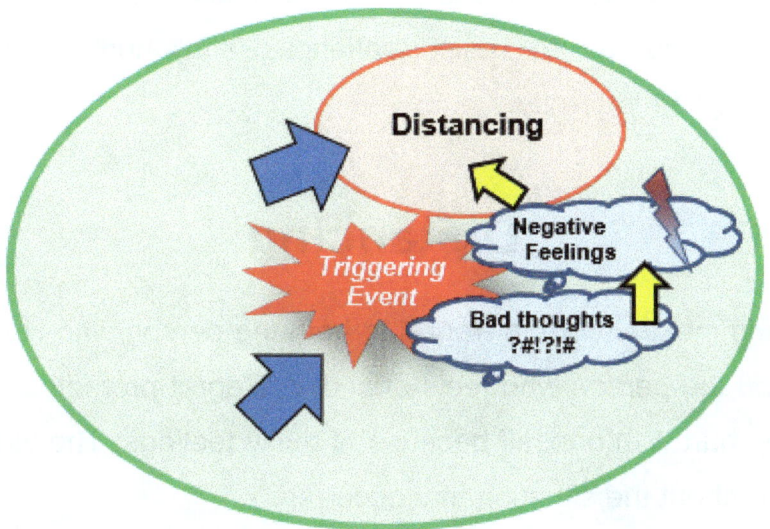

Triggering Event

Material temptations (ambition) or powerful impulses that instigate a person to act maliciously towards another person or group of people can motivate events that trigger conflict.

A stimulus or force (impetus) prompts the inner movement of the irresistible will to act, sometimes in an uncontrolled and thoughtless way, against another person. For example, feelings of jealousy.

People have inherent impulses and temptations that are automatically acted upon with ill intentions, leading to problems that serve as tests to be conquered.

To minimize impulses and temptations, it is essential to maintain good spirits, the courage to resist, patience, faith, humility, goodwill, forgiveness and fraternity.

Distancing

Distancing makes room for regret to both the person who caused the event and the person who feels offended. Regret promotes the state of feeling hurt with oneself because of guilty feelings. The victim also feels bad about the situation that occurred.

This component aims to promote psychological and physical distancing (if possible) between the offender, the offended person, and the unpleasant scene when the event occurred. For example, arguments, fight, disagreement, discord or rudeness.

To minimize the mental connection between the offender and the victim, it becomes necessary to put distance between them. Typically, this connection arises through "mental dialogues" that frequently pulse from the unconscious mind and transmit feelings of hatred, sadness, revenge, resentment, and hurt.

The act of distancing oneself psychically gives space for the conscious mind to exercise the powers of thought to create alternatives for life. Disconnecting from the problem means stopping to feed oneself with "*What If's and If Only's*" and negative emotions. In short, we stop vibrating our minds in the same attunement and direction as others, returning to intimate vital contact. This is the positive attitude of exiting the victim's position.

Bearing in mind that, because the effort to overcome hurt aims at preserving health, it becomes necessary to redirect our thinking to something positive. It is healthy to disconnect from unpleasant (toxic) facts and people. The techniques described below can help assuage the bitterness of the mind.

> 1. *Write a note to yourself.*
>
> Describe the event and people's attitudes during that time.
>
> The act of writing leads us to reflect on what happened in more detail. As a result, it assuages the negative feelings of the mind and heart. After reflecting on what you wrote, it is advisable to destroy it, preferably by burning it. Employ this technique when the mind feels burdened by problematic memories.
>
> 2. *Cut the connection with the offender or offended party.*

When a disturbing event comes to mind, try to detach yourself from it by focusing your thoughts on the activity that you are currently carrying out. This means keeping your mind occupied with something useful and safe. It is difficult, but not impossible.

The practice of concentration helps you train yourself to cut off connections that are interfering with your daily life. Concentration involves maintaining high-level thoughts with short-wave frequencies (Chapter 5, sub-title Attunement).

3. *Reflect on what motivates aggressive behavior.*

You may discover how you contributed to the unpleasant event. This reflection is important for identifying and improving your own habits and attitudes.

For the offender, reflection leads to regret, which is the feeling of remorse, a fundamental part of realizing the mistake you made. To regret is to feel hurt by the mistake you made or the negative attitudes you practiced.

For the victim, remorse also leads to regret for having spent energy and suffering for a perceived reason that caused the offense, even if it was a one-off situation.

Compassion comprises forgiveness and forgetting the offense. Compassion elevates the soul and helps to ease negative emotions in the relationship between the offender and the victim.

When choosing to forgive someone, keep in mind that you must plan and practice forgiveness humbly, without aggressiveness, with the heart and generosity. Forgiveness is an act of benevolence and does not imply creating humiliating conditions for the other party. Without generosity on both sides, reconciliation becomes very difficult.

In Christianity and Judaism, repentance is equivalent to the rejection of unacceptable behavior and the consequent intention of no longer practicing it. This form of regret leads the person to want to change their attitudes.

To reflect...

1. What is the benefit of distancing oneself after a disagreement?

2. Describe the techniques that can disconnect you from the event that occurred.

10. Regeneration

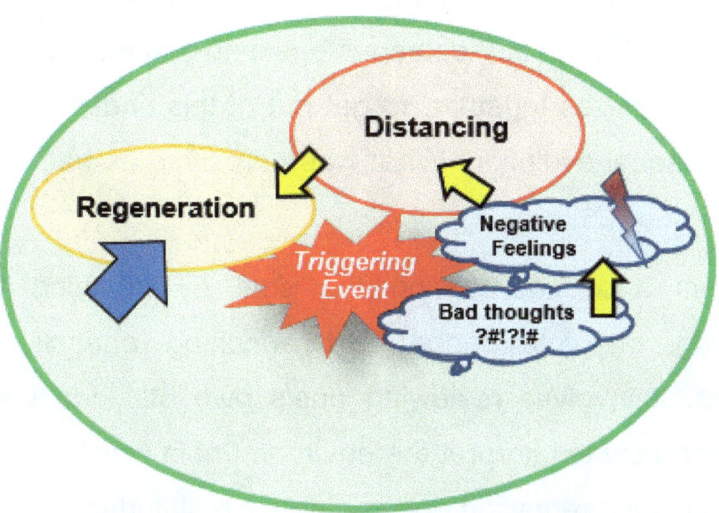

Regeneration involves physical and moral suffering, equivalent to penance to ease guilt. Sacred texts describe a series of expiatory sacrifices to show repentance for improper acts committed.

This stage demands more time, effort, and changes in the habits and inappropriate behaviors that contributed to the triggering event or recurring situations.

Human values include efforts to accept and transform bad habits into good ones, while respecting one's own limits and those of others.

Mere words or promises are insufficient. True repentance works on deep feelings, such as hurt, bitterness, sadness, anger, anxiety, anguish, pity, compassion, and disappointment.

The scenario of bitterness, of reaching "rock bottom", comes to mind. This is the point when self-esteem steps in to make the person get up and pull themselves together, to get out of this undesirable situation through personal evolution. What was perceived as bad will become good!

Learning is about developing the soul by purifying the mind, enlightening the intelligence and enriching oneself with new knowledge. It involves reviewing one's own attitudes towards life, reflecting on how to interpret the environment in which one lives and, finally, embracing renewing and constructive attitudes.

To become conscious

One pillar of renewal is awareness of the event that caused the problem. Consciousness is the faculty of reason, the capacity to judge one's own actions with impartiality. It brings about the feeling of remorse and sincerity. Through consciousness, we think, observe, and interact with the outside world.

Consciousness defines the attribute that moves between reason and sensitivity (Head-Heart). It is the secret voice of the soul that lives within us and guides us towards the path of good, based on compassion and the practice of love.

"*Staying conscious*" uses reason, the ability to process the facts experienced with logic, being able to think and be aware of physical and mental actions.

"*Being conscious*" is no longer a momentary state of existence, referring to our way of existing in the world. It connects to the way we lead our lives and our ability to establish emotional connections with people and things, such as our ability to love.

The will to "*become conscious*" of reality is fundamental. People often live without truly experiencing their own reality. They survive without their own determination; they become dependent and are easily influenced by other people. In short, they are not masters of their mental states, and this affects their free will and individual progress.

Changing habits and attitudes

Habit is the usual way of being or acting. Toxic feelings are mental attitudes that compel the individual to control people and situations.

Parents and adults should avoid instilling negative and misleading messages in children, as these tend to create fear and block their development. Their sense of autonomy and independence becomes affected and such messages continue to be harmful in adulthood.

Indecisive, insecure, and fearful adults end up being more prone to developing addictions and manias because of the fear of taking control and responsibility for their actions and attitudes.

We see adults with insecure and prejudiced attitudes, such as:

- Abusive use of alcohol, sex, nicotine, drugs and gambling as momentary compensations for the fragile and unstructured soul.
- Gluttony, or toxic feelings about eating, becomes an "escape option".
- Mania of talking uncontrollably, constantly lying and often positioning oneself as a victim, always thinking oneself right, unnecessary spending, criticizing, judging others and working compulsively.

Deactivating harmful habits

To begin, we consider addictions and toxic feelings, bad habits, not sins. They are compulsive disorders, and science has uncovered their respective mechanisms and solutions. In addition, they serve as a means for us to overcome our trials and challenges that can make us better.

We must always question our attitudes. For example:

a. Question our own habits.
b. Minimize interference by making our own decisions.

c. Fight the tendency to be "nice".

d. Stimulate the ability to say "no" to develop a sense of autonomy.

e. Eliminate relationships of overdependence so as not to feel suffocated.

f. Create positive behavior patterns for life situations.

g. Exercise free will as a liberated human being who is in control of his or her actions and thoughts.

h. Develop self-knowledge, the benefit of which is to accept one's "inadequate" attitudes and improve them.

We know that a powerful message received systematically imprints physically on neurons, forming habits. Neurons become accustomed to these impressions and end up forming a permanent pathway of transmission from neuron to neuron.

The graph below shows the habit cycle. The compulsive disorder (trigger) leads to the execution of something habitual. Once triggered, the person takes the action of executing the habit, and then feels rewarded (relief).

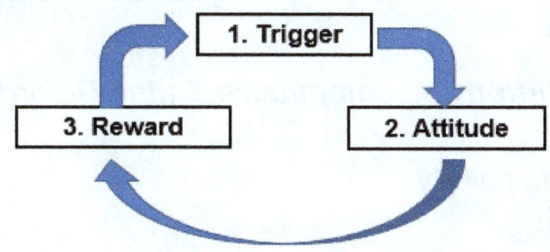

To deactivate these mental impressions, it is necessary to maintain a proactive and disciplined stance in the following way:

  a. Perceive and identify negative habits.

  b. Understand each habit through in-depth analysis, trying to discover whether it is associated with any other factor.

  c. Describe new attitudes and desired compensations.

  d. Memorize them.

Changing habits is often a hard task to accomplish, but not impossible. In extreme cases, it is advisable to seek the help of health professionals and therapists.

Let's look at the example below, which triggers the habit of gobbling quickly.

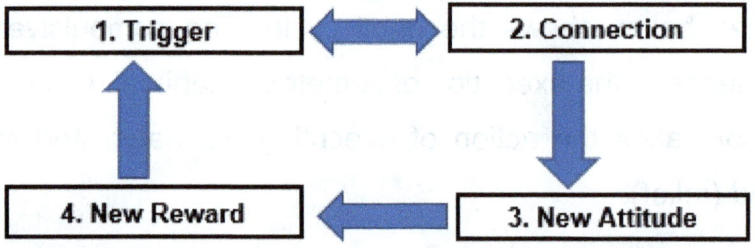

Gluttony or Compulsive Eating Disorder

1. Trigger. Eating quickly.

2. Connection. Desire to eat a lot and finish quickly associated with the following factors:

   a. Frequent messages in childhood to "clean the plate".

   b. As an adult, he/she performed other activities during mealtimes. Because of the pressure of time, he/she stopped paying attention to the meal and chewing quickly became a habit.

   c. Previous attitude: Finish eating quickly, clean the plate and feel satisfied.

   d. Previous reward: full stomach and complete satisfaction.

3. New attitude. Before starting the meal:

   a. Just relax and appreciate the food.

   b. Observe the food and not the plate.

   c. Tasting: recognizing the food that is being eaten.

   d. Add a small quantity of food to your mouth.

   e. Return the cutlery to the plate while chewing at least 20 times before swallowing.

4. New reward:

   Better digestion and less drowsiness.

   A feeling of victory and well-being.

To reflect...

1. Do you have any bad habits that need changing? Using the method described above, how do you plan to correct them?

2. Describe the three conscious states:

>   *"Staying conscious"*

>   *"Being conscious"*

>   *"Become conscious"*

11. Reparation

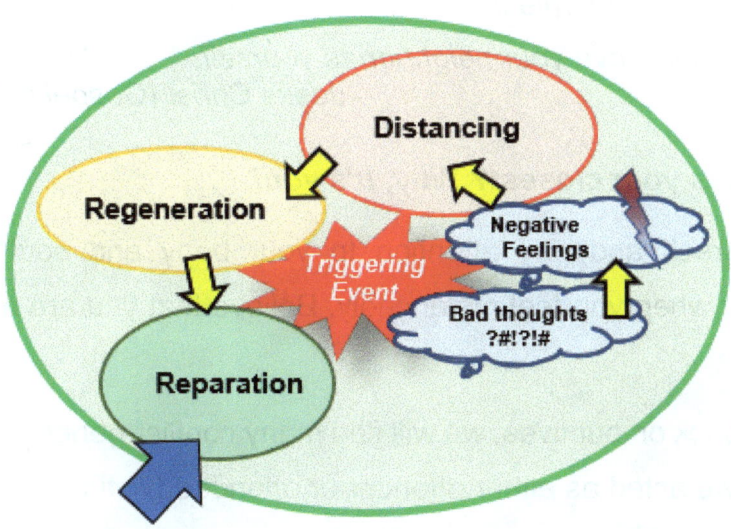

Through Reparation, we can minimize the effects of the event that caused the problem. This stage includes retracting yourself, compensating for the damage caused, and sincerely apologizing.

The importance of reparation is to free oneself from "captivity" (suffering) through obtaining forgiveness, changing attitudes, and doing good to the harmed person.

Love thy neighbor...

Keep in mind the following quotes:

> "Forgiveness is an absolute necessity for the continuation of human existence." - Desmond Tutu, Bishop in South Africa

*"Lord, ... For it is in giving that we receive.
It is in pardoning that we are pardoned..."*
- Prayer of St. Francis

"Love your enemies!"

"You shall love your neighbor as yourself. "
- Jesus Christ (Gospel of Matthew)

And who is your closest? Why, it's you!

Love yourself and pay attention to your body and soul function, especially when you feel melancholy. Believe that you are a precious person!

Looking back on our lives, we will find many conflict-generating events in which we acted as either offender or offended (victims).

As offenders, we would love to be forgiven by our victims. Right?

We should not interpret the statement "Love your enemies!" literally, because the feeling of affection we have for our friends is not the same for those who are our adversaries.

Having affection for an enemy is extremely difficult. For our own benefit, it is better to stop holding grudges, hatred, and desire for revenge, even if there is no chance of reconciliation.

In the event of reconciliation, adversaries forgive each other without obstacles and with no intention of humiliating the other one.

In short, forgive while wishing the best for others. Forgiveness frees the soul, protects health, and prevents psychosomatic illnesses.

We must repair our mistakes as soon as possible so as not to perpetuate the problem. Suffering brings harm to the entire organism, starting with psychosomatic illnesses and affecting the endocrine glands, the nervous system, and other organs.

We know of many cases of people who, at the end of their lives, ask their adversaries to come to them so they can be forgiven. Don't let resentment and hatred follow you to the grave. For spiritualists, this means avoiding possible obsessions in future lives.

Repairing mistakes is an opportunity to progress morally. The offender can directly remedy the physical or moral harm caused to the victim by asking for forgiveness, changing his or her attitude and replacing the damaged material goods.

The meaning of the act of making amends is profound, as it involves repairing, compensating for losses and making amends for the offended person.

If the victim does not accept the request for forgiveness, the offender can make amends by volunteering or performing good deeds for the offended party, which resolves the issue and relieves feelings. It is a conscious way of resolving the issue and relieving feelings.

Reparation elevates the soul, making us more humble, charitable, and helpful.

An example of citizenship and simple reparation is the note that a lady left on the windshield of my car. She wrote:

> *"The wind blew into my car. The door opened and marked your passenger side door. Please call me on 999-9999. Sorry about this."*

This stranger took responsibility for the damage caused. I called her to thank her for such a noble gesture.

A curious case occurred in August 2022 in the state of Espírito Santo (Brazil). A man who stole a car regretted it after seeing a modified child's seat in the back of the car. He returned the car with a full tank of gas and an apology note that read:

> *"The crime asks for forgiveness. During the rush of it, the child's problem was not seen. I am returning the car with a full tank!*

There are countless examples of reparation. One of the most important was the Catholic Church's retraction to indigenous Canadians: dozens of graves with the remains of indigenous children were found in the backyards of Catholic ethnic boarding schools in Canadian Provinces.

To reflect...

1. Do you love yourself?

2. If you have adversaries, can you at least respect them as people?

12. Meditation

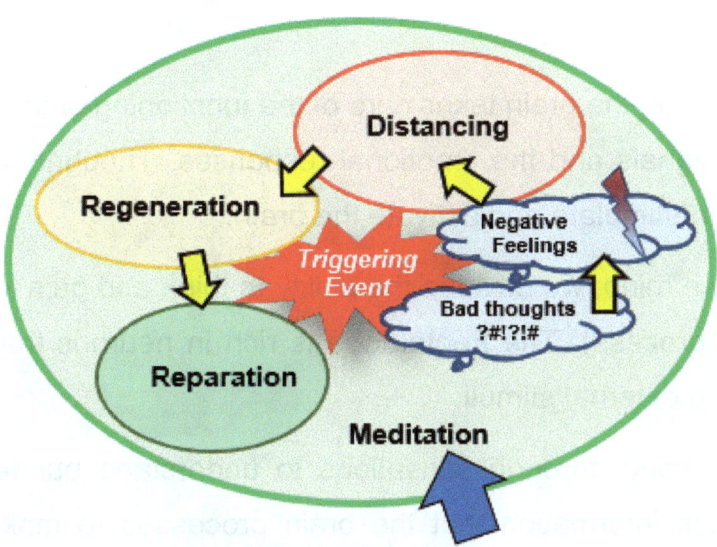

Meditation brings together and supports the other components. It accompanies the entire process until forgiveness and healing of suffering occur. Suffering can result from guilt for offending someone, being offended, or being involved in undesirable situations.

By practicing meditation, we actively review and improve the components of this process. We exercise the faculty of thinking by generating ideas and thoughts, which we can then select based on the actions required to follow our choices. I suggest reviewing the chapter "Our Choices" where you can find detailed information on the subject.

The mind contains various thoughts, often in a disorderly manner. Meditation helps us review these thoughts, organize them, and define one that expresses the principle or purpose we wish to achieve. We can call it a "key thought" to guide the solution to the problem under analysis.

While we think, the brain takes care of the functioning of the body, the electrical signals and the emotional responses. Thoughts generated by the mind stimulate and activate the brain.

Through the mind, we develop the ability to think and gain knowledge (cognitive process). The frontal lobe is rich in neurons that process internal and external stimuli.

The mind works through sensations to understand our feelings. It accumulates information that the brain processes to make our life possible. Therefore, human beings can choose between "suffering" and "not suffering".

As described in the chapter Psychosomatic Diseases, the brain is the physical part in the head that takes care of the functioning of the body. It acts through thoughts generated by the mind.

The Mind is abstract and immaterial. It has no shape, weight, measurement, or physical location. It reveals our ability to think and gain knowledge. There are three types of minds:

Higher Mind. It connects with the Universe and spirituality through the energies that emanate from the crown chakra, influenced by thought, which is composed of magnetic energies (fluids).

The higher mind provides the transformative energies we need to prosper. It has abundant resources to make our dreams and desires come true.

Conscious Mind. It processes logical reasoning, imagines, solves problems and works on positive thoughts.

The conscious mind coordinates the mental mechanism. It defines objectives, filters information, maintains control over other minds, elaborates and decides desires.

Unconscious Mind. The conscious mind influences it. It keeps files of memories, impressions, feelings, behaviors, and all positive and negative vibrations.

The process of forgiving someone begins with analyzing the negative feelings rooted in the unconscious mind.

Through willpower, meditation and therapy, it is possible to transform these negative feelings into positive ones, as illustrated below.

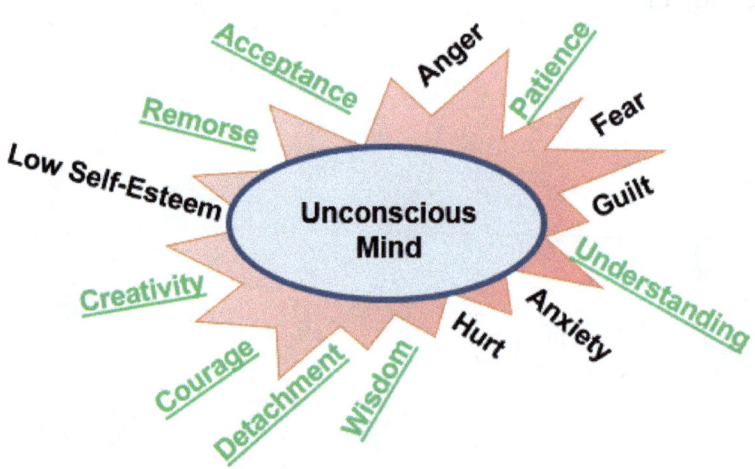

Alignment of minds

Misaligned minds lack harmony among them and give rise to feelings of low self-esteem, fear, barriers to forgiveness, etc.

The unconscious mind is not proactive. It pulses frequently, releasing illogical feelings and ideas. For example, sometimes we speak or act and, soon after, we realize that we did so "without thinking".

The lack of harmony among the minds favors the simple reproduction of messages released by the unconscious mind without prior rational analysis by the conscious mind. So, we speak and act without thinking.

The practice of meditation is the ideal way to maintain alignment and harmony among the minds. Through it, we can clear unwanted memories that are fixed in the unconscious mind, providing clarity, prosperity, and consequent happiness in life.

Analyze this situation of misaligned minds following the numerical sequence.

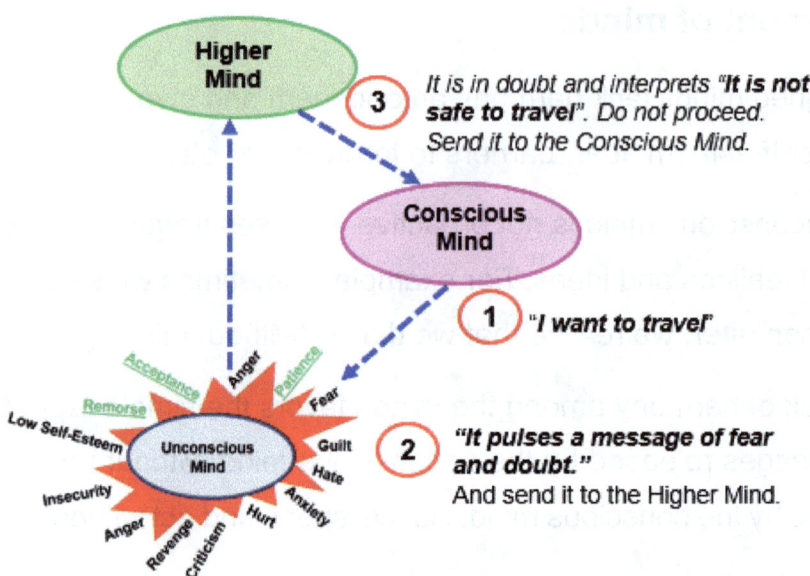

The proper alignment of minds promotes a vibrational state that allows us to materialize dreams and desires.

The graph below reproduces the example above with minds aligned and in tune.

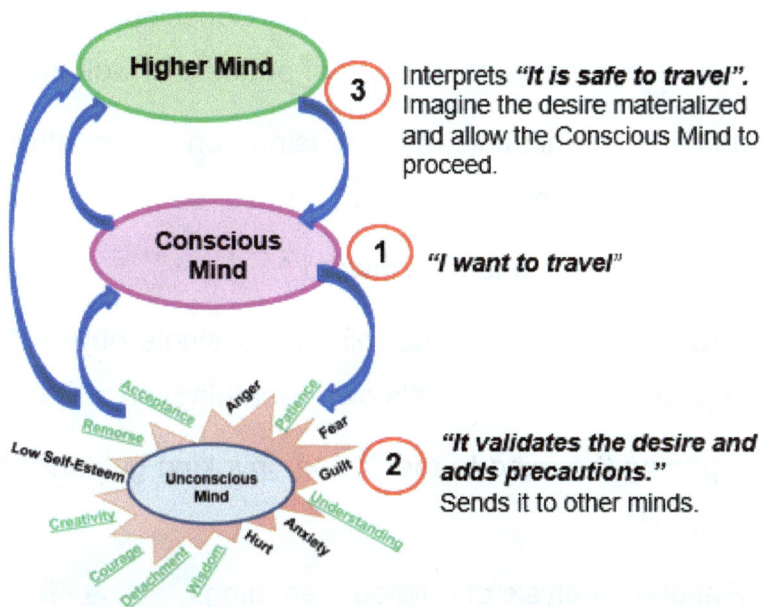

Meditating

"We are not human beings having a spiritual experience; we are spiritual beings having a human experience."

— Pierre Teilhard de Chardin

We emit wave bands called frequencies. Beta wave band (14 to 21 cycles/second) is the frequency when we are awake, and the mind is prepared to perform tasks that require attention.

Alpha wave band is suitable for meditation because the vibrational waves are slow (less than 14 cycles/second). The person can have their eyes closed, with their senses partially asleep, but in a relaxed and pre-sleep state (deep relaxation). Consciousness expands, flowing creative energies and feelings of peace and well-being.

People practice meditation by focusing on concentration and contemplation. Examples:

    a. "Turning one's attention inward."

    b. Practice of focusing the mind on a single object. Ex.: on a religious statue, on one's own breathing, on a mantra.

    c. Opening the mind to the Divine, invoking guidance from the highest.

    d. Rational analysis of religious teachings.

Attention and Concentration

The only limits to your mind are those you believe you have! Attention is the action of focusing your soul on something. It precedes concentration and they work together.

Concentration is an intense form of attention. The amplitude depends on the person's biological conditions, their physical and mental well-being, the time of day, what is happening in their life, and their interest in completing the task. For example, each person has their own biological clock. Some feel more alert in the morning, others during the evening.

Through thought, you can direct your attention to a person or scene.

a. If you know the person, your mind immediately brings up their image.

b. If you have a vague knowledge of the person, your mind needs a reference (photo or picture).

c. If you don't know the person, your mind needs spiritual help to locate them.

It is common for us to perform boring tasks we want to finish quickly. Positive motivation and self-reward can ease the task.

Practicing concentration

There are several techniques for practicing relaxation and concentration. Books, videos, and social media offer several techniques for practicing relaxation and concentration.

For example, individuals can practice concentration by using the mental image of a candle flame to reduce the influx of distracting thoughts, enhancing their well-being and mindfulness. Being in this calm state can mentally energize all the organs of the body.

These exercises follow the following steps:
    1. Preparing the body
    2. Practicing relaxation
    3. Practicing concentration
    4. Returning to the normal state

Practicing concentration is very beneficial when we are praying. Prayer is self-help! It doesn't matter what your religion or creed is. The simple act of elevating your thoughts and meditating on your life and your attitudes restores the peace and serenity that you so desperately need.

To request forgiveness from God, we must renew our attitudes to overcome bad habits.

Praying for protection is not enough. It is necessary to be vigilant, stay awake, observe and remain attentive to us and to surrounding people. We need to discern, compare, induce, deduce, and judge what is around us. To perceive beyond appearances, to discern between true and false.

Prayer is the act of connecting with God and can have as its object a request, a thank you, or praise.

Prayer is an invocation and a mental relationship with the Being we are addressing. This is possible because the universal fluid surrounds us (chapter The Body Speaks and Writes!).

Willpower to fulfill a request drives the fluid that is the agent of thought. Through prayer, we can boost the energies of health, courage, patience and resignation to the person to whom we are addressing.

Besides will, faith and merit are essential elements. Magnetic action directly responds to the power of faith by affecting the body's fluids and transforming their properties.

Having genuine faith means we possess an unwavering desire and conviction that our wishes will be fulfilled. The absence of faith lacks the fundamental catalyst for healing.

To reflect...

1. List at least two benefits of practicing meditation.

2. Describe the functions of the Higher, Conscious, and Unconscious minds.

3. Think of a desire and practice aligning your minds for two minutes, as explained above.

13. Self-Forgiveness

"You can't go back and make a new start, but you can start right now and make a brand-new ending."
- *James R. Sherman*

Self-forgiveness is one of the fundamental elements of a good life. It involves changing attitudes throughout life and accepting who we are without prejudging ourselves. Self-forgiveness is part of the conscious evolution of human beings, bringing to light what is true about themselves.

In unpleasant situations, particularly during childhood and youth, we often struggle to understand our role, especially when we experience mistreatment or abandonment. The lack of clear understanding of the events that occurred causes feelings of guilt, remorse and resentment that remain latent throughout life and need to be resolved.

It is common for us to take ourselves as a point of reference and end up considering other human beings as fragile or "abnormal". Through the feeling of compassion, we can "put on their clothes" and analyze our own depths. Those we consider "abnormal" are our mirrors, our shadows.

Because of these characteristics, self-forgiveness involves analyzing the mistakes we made or the angry emotions we held. It also requires a deep analysis of the upbringing we received. Many lessons learned in the past are inadequate for the current personal goal of peace, harmony, prosperity, and happiness.

The significant benefit of self-forgiveness is the opportunity to begin the inner reform that is so necessary if we are to achieve the freedom to think and act responsibly.

Internal conflicts need to be reviewed to learn how to deal with them. Censoring, perfectionism, self-demand, and routines can be relaxed. We must change or even eliminate prejudices and their paradigms through the exercise of meditation.

Freedom of thought brings about the reevaluation of religious dogmas imprinted in our memory and that still generates doubts, prejudices, and false sensations of non-existent sins.

We must make interpretations of biblical passages, dogmas, and religious beliefs according to the time in which we live. Always avoid literal understanding because people wrote those texts centuries ago. They reflect the sociopolitical and religious context of that time.

With effort, we can extract religious teachings that enlighten our conscience with healthy and non-terrifying behaviors. By adopting this ideal approach, we can bring light to identifying many misleading statements that have been passed down to us and led us to believe blindly.

What is important to achieve self-forgiveness is to stop living in the past. To renew ourselves so we can live in the present and the future, keeping God in our hearts.

You may feel a slight discomfort with your self-esteem during the self-analysis process. Our failure to accept ourselves as people causes low self-esteem. We forget that besides the toxic feelings we admit to having; we have many good feelings to offer. Self-acceptance reaffirms our individuality and makes us feel secure in ourselves.

In conclusion, self-forgiveness frees us from the guilt we carry, and which blocks our evolution. It frees us from the anchors that keep us trapped in unnecessary captivity and prevent us from exercising our right to prosper and be happy. We can now recognize the abundance that Divinity offers us.

Driving Self-Forgiveness Deeper

All religions have prayers for forgiveness. For this exercise, take a prayer from your religion or belief that deals with forgiveness.

For example, I took the Lord's Prayer, known to Christians, as the basis for this analysis. It reads:

> *"Forgive us our trespasses,*
> *as we forgive those who trespass against us."*

Every offense generates debt. Do we sincerely want to pay off this debt? Depending on the severity of the offense, we are powerless to forgive. Then, we appeal to divine mercy. But does God forget everything? Or is it our conscience that does not forget?

The usual wording of this prayer uses the pronoun in the first-person plural (we). The commitment to God gets diluted and distributed throughout the community. It gives the impression that if I cannot commit to forgiving, someone in the community can do it for me.

Now reread the same prayer in the first-person singular (I):

> *"Forgive me <u>my</u> trespasses,*
> *as <u>I</u> forgive those who trespass against <u>me</u>."*

When we think in the first-person singular, we are more aware of the intention this phrase awakens. It has a deeper effect; moves us deeply; commits and motivates us to reevaluate the offenses so that they no longer interfere with our lives.

Lack of forgiveness is disturbing and takes the focus away from daily activities. Lack of forgiveness often attunes us to the offenders, or victims, generating resentment, hurt, anger, hatred, desire for revenge and psychosomatic illnesses.

And what is the measure of forgiveness? As the gospels say, our commitment measures forgiveness. It is proportional to how we take responsibility. Without my forgiveness, there is no forgiveness to me.

Now, what can I do for myself?

Based on the guidelines described in this book, if you are suffering, these directions can guide your life from now on:

* Renew your attitudes
* Pray and be vigilant!

Renew your attitudes

a. *Discover your best good feelings*

Trying to renew your attitudes by focusing on vices and toxic feelings, or even on your faults, is a difficult and frustrating task. The most appropriate strategy is to identify your relevant good feelings and improve them. Thus, you will gradually rectify and diminish the significance of undesirable habits.

b. *Divine Laws*

They look after your individual progress. All creatures in this world have developed, adapted, and are making progress. You will also progress through your effort and self-reward.

c. *Reasoned faith*

Be kind to yourself and desire change. You may be inhibiting this desire to progress deep within yourself. Make sure you fulfill this desire.

d. *Thought*

We can emit positive and negative vibrations. Change your way of thinking by bringing optimism into your life. Stop keeping your thoughts anchored in unpleasant facts.

e. *Acceptance*

Accept life's calls for inner renewal.

Pray and be vigilant!

We must always watch ourselves to avoid keeping our thoughts anchored in unpleasant situations.
The best way to keep ourselves focused on good things is through prayer, as they nourish us with courage, patience and resignation. Prayers inspire us to overcome difficulties on our own merit.

Prayers addressed to guardian angels, or guardian spirits, inspire good thoughts, bring the necessary moral strength to overcome difficulties and ward off the evils that we attract through our carelessness.

To reflect...

1. Do you remember any offense or conflict that needs your forgiveness? When examining this scenario, ask yourself: "Did I create this conflict? Or did I influence or facilitate this conflict to happen?"

2. Do you feel flexible enough to change your habits? Reflect on two habits that could impede your growth. How can you change them?

3. "Now, what can I do for myself?"

   Reflect on this question. Consider actions that will refresh attitudes and stay on the path of goodness.

Part IV

Conclusions

Congratulations! You are about to finish reading this book and are ready to put the knowledge you gained into practice.

Right at the beginning, we stated that practicing forgiveness in a conscious and objective way is necessary to eliminate negative feelings that affect physical and mental health.

Forgiveness is one component of the group of good feelings, which also includes humility, freedom, acceptance, compassion, detachment and wisdom.

We outlined an overview of the causes of external and internal conflicts. They are important sources to be observed so that we can live with divergent situations.

Because our choice is to progress in life, we need to guard ourselves against situations and messages that take our focus away from our personal goals.

Illnesses often originate in the mind before manifesting in the body's organs. We can change this situation by activating positive thoughts and feelings that drive healthy fluids to the cells and energy centers.

The body speaks and writes! It expresses itself, commanded by the head, which holds important glands, the brain and the mind. Together, they make this divine engineering that we use to live function.

Forgiving is not a fleeting and general decision. It is impossible for us to forgive and be forgiven for all our mistakes simultaneously. The process of forgiving involves understanding life and the environment in which we live. Through the school of life, we receive lessons on how to live in peace with other beings and try to be happy.

We also deal with changes in habits that require effort, sacrifice, perseverance, and action. Forgiveness is a resource for personal change and health. People with illness show improvements after resolving their interpersonal issues through forgiveness.

Self-forgiveness breaks down the barriers that impede spiritual progress. Its practice brings the benefit of reestablishing intimate contact with our own individuality. Feelings of security and determination emerge. This way, we feel strong enough to avoid getting involved in situations that pose the risk of making us into victims.

The process of forgiving and transforming oneself is ongoing. The difficulties observed reflect human weaknesses. To minimize their suffering, people need to be encouraged to adopt the habit of self-analysis. This way, they can avoid feeling like victims and become proactive people and develop their capacities (mental, emotional and spiritual). This is what the Creator expects from human beings.

We can teach the Cycle of Forgiveness to children and young people so that they learn to protect themselves against the suffering caused by sources of conflict.

Practicing the Cycle of Forgiveness brings the following benefits:

    a. It promotes the release from suffering.

    b. It helps in the treatment of psychological disorders.

    c. It heals memories of painful experiences.

    d. It detoxifies feelings of guilt, fear, hurt, resentment, anger, frustration, and anxiety.

    e. It helps to identify bad or inappropriate habits.

    f. It helps to discover the reasons that lead us to play both the roles of offenders and offended (victims).

Treatment success relies on patient determination and effort. Memorize the diagram below0,0 as it is a good and effective way to heal your suffering.

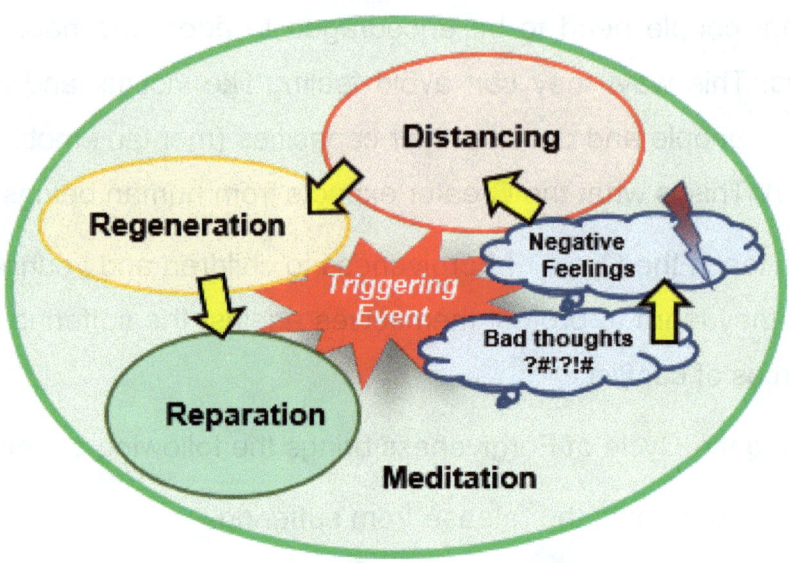

To reflect...

Live and don't be ashamed of being happy.

Sing, and sing, and sing

The beauty of being an eternal learner."

- "What Is It, What Is It?" song - Gonzaguinha

Part V

Frequently Asked Questions

Forgiveness and a world in turmoil.

"The world is in turmoil, causing much suffering to the entire population. How can we handle forgiveness in such a situation?

Throughout history, conflicts arose because of the pursuit of power, land conquest, and territorial defense.

It is not possible for us to solve the world's problems, much less blame ourselves for the suffering that others are going through. We must improve ourselves and inspire others towards goodness.

Even when we witness this general suffering, we should meditate and try to act to soothe those who suffer. You can contribute by volunteering or fervently praying.

Can the Cycle of Forgiveness interfere with treatments?

"I am undergoing treatment with a therapist to heal some mental symptoms that I have been experiencing. Can the proposed Cycle of Forgiveness interfere with the treatment?"

Good question. The purpose of the Cycle of Forgiveness is to help people understand the environment in which they live and the components that affect their health. Forgiveness is a healing therapy with no contraindications.

The Cycle of Forgiveness and our dark side.

"I read that one of our problems today is that we deny our dark side and try to become completely good. Isn't the Cycle of Forgiveness a way of denying our dark side?"

Practicing the Cycle of Forgiveness helps to clarify our dark side by renewing attitudes so we can face life with clarity and purpose.

The Cycle of Forgiveness and religious beliefs.

"Can people of any religious belief and atheists use the proposed Cycle of Forgiveness?"

Yes. Forgiveness is a health issue, not a religious precept. The proposed *Cycle of Forgiveness* is based on science. The attitude of forgiveness is compatible with all religious beliefs.

Each person follows their beliefs and can include their own ways of praying during the practice. By resolving their issues, people can more easily adhere to their beliefs.

"I have read religious books that deal with forgiveness. Why doesn't the Cycle of Forgiveness emphasize religion?"

There are many books that deal with forgiveness from the point of view of religious dogmas and principles. However, they are not explicit about how to forgive.

The *Cycle of Forgiveness* focuses on the diversity of people, regardless of creed. It only seeks to answer the question "How to forgive?" with emphasis on health.

I believe that the sincere practice of forgiveness becomes a healthy personal habit of any individual human.

Atheism and forgiveness.

"I don't believe in God, and I don't believe in karma either. So why should I forgive someone?"

As we've said, forgiveness is a question of health and not of belief. The question of believing in God comes with time and life experiences.

Relationship between evil and forgiveness.

"Do you believe that there is such a thing as evil in the world? What is the relationship between evil and forgiveness?"

Let's analyze it this way: evil exists because God allows it to exist.

The evil deeds committed by human beings generate pain that needs to be overcome. They are trials that we can use to grow morally. Remember: "we grow through love or through pain!"

Is there anything we should not forgive?

"In my opinion, there are unforgivable things that should never be forgiven."

Who are we to judge what can be forgiven?

If we suffer, there is reason to meditate on this pain and try to discover its cause. When pain reaches our feelings, the best way out is to free ourselves through forgiveness.

The Cycle of Forgiveness versus size of the faults.

"I understand that the proposed Cycle of Forgiveness is for relatively minor situations. Regarding serious offenses such as rape and murder, what are your thoughts? Should we forgive them?"

The proposed solution aims to be adaptable to any level of gravity, and individuals should seek the help of a health professional for serious cases.

When an unpleasant event occurs, we immediately cry out for justice. Even the courts grant full forgiveness in certain cases or reduce the sentence oftentimes.

Although the guilty party also suffers, the injured party suffers a lot and needs support and a way to lessen their pain and free themselves from the bonds of anger. Practicing the proposed path leads to this goal.

The Cycle of Forgiveness and addictions.

"I am an alcoholic, and I continue to drink. Even though I have this addiction, can I use your proposal?"

Of course. You are a human being, and you probably feel guilty about having this addiction and the unpleasant consequences that affect your loved ones. Without a doubt, you can use the proposed path as therapy.

The Cycle of Forgiveness and gluttony.

"I have a problem with food. I suffer from gluttony, and I feel guilty about it."

Scientific articles reveal that gluttony – the habit of overeating – is not a sin, as religions prescribe. A lack of emotional control over food and other toxic feelings is at the root.

Experts acknowledge gluttony as a compulsive eating disorder driven by unconscious suffering. Besides excess weight, gluttony results in feelings of guilt and shame. Gluttony has a cure through changing habits and therapies. You can use the proposed path without limits to get rid of the guilt caused by gluttony.

The Cycle of Forgiveness and Sexual Orientation.

"Doesn't the proposed path deal with sexual orientation?"

The Cycle of Forgiveness aims to help people, regardless of sexual orientation, to free themselves from their pain through forgiveness.

Difficulty in forgiving.

"I have difficulty forgiving my situation. I can forgive people, but I'm going through difficult times, and I find it difficult to forgive myself."

Precisely in difficult times, we must meditate more to find our inner self and the solution to get out of the situation. Depending on the severity, you may need to seek medical and psychological help.

Forgiveness and success.

"Can forgiveness make me successful?"

Yes, absolutely. We interpret success in terms of love, money, status and power, with the consequent ostentation. Forgiveness has no connection to these terms. By freeing oneself from suffering, one's attention turns to one's inner self and, therefore, acquires the chance to embark on projects where one can exercise one's talents freely.

Forgiveness and karma.

"If I practice forgiveness, will I be able to eliminate my bad karma?"

In Sanskrit, karma means "action". According to your personal values, karma can be positive or negative, depending on your free will to think and act.

If you think negatively, try to discover the reason through meditation. You will discover the origin (generating event) of this behavior that you call "bad karma". We know that each generating event is associated with some unpleasant fact that demands an attitude of forgiveness.

Forgiveness and age limits.

"Is there an age limit you would recommend for forgiving?"

There is no age limit for forgiving. It is important for individuals to seek healing from suffering at any time and not wait until their deathbed. It makes no sense to suffer your whole life, only to ask someone for forgiveness at the last minute.

And now?

*Go forward
with faith,
will,
hope,
perseverance,
vigilance
and love!*

Brotherly hug!

Erson

www.ingramcontent.com/pod-product-compliance
Lightning Source LLC
Chambersburg PA
CBHW070606050426
42450CB00011B/3006